Unsung Heroes

THE AZRIELI SERIES OF HOLOCAUST SURVIVOR MEMOIRS: PUBLISHED TITLES

ENGLISH TITLES

Unsung Heroes
Tibor (Zvi) Benyovits

THE AZRIELI FOUNDATION
www.azrielifoundation.org

Cover and book design by Mark Goldstein
Endpaper maps by Martin Gilbert
Map on page xxvii by François Blanc
Cover image courtesy of Archiv für Zeitgeschichte ETH Zürich / Agnes Hirschi

LIBRARY AND ARCHIVES CANADA CATALOGUING IN PUBLICATION

Benyovits, Tibor, 1932–, author
    Unsung Heroes/ Tibor Benyovits.

(Azrieli series of Holocaust survivor memoirs. Series x)
Includes index.
ISBN 978-1-988065-32-8 (softcover) · 8 7 6 5 4 3 2 1

1. Benyovits, Tibor, 1932–. 2. Jews — Hungary — Budapest — Biography. 3. Noar ha-Tsiyoni (Organization: Hungary). 4. World War, 1939–1945 — Jewish resistance — Hungary — Budapest. 5. Holocaust, Jewish (1939–1945) — Hungary — Budapest. 6. Budapest (Hungary) — History. 7. Jews, Hungarian — Israel — Biography. 8. Jews — Canada — Biography. 9. Autobiographies. I. Azrieli Foundation, issuing body II. Title.

DS135.H93B46 2018   940.53'1832092   C2018-901910-7

MIX
Paper from
responsible sources
FSC® C004191
www.fsc.org

PRINTED IN CANADA

The Azrieli Series of Holocaust Survivor Memoirs

Naomi Azrieli, Publisher

Jody Spiegel, Program Director
Arielle Berger, Managing Editor
Matt Carrington, Editor
Devora Levin, Assistant Editor
Elizabeth Lasserre, Senior Editor, French-Language Editions
Elin Beaumont, Senior Education Outreach and Program Facilitator
Catherine Person, Bilingual Education and Outreach Coordinator
Stephanie Corazza, Education and Curriculum Associate
Marc-Olivier Cloutier, Bilingual Educational Outreach and Events
    Assistant
Elizabeth Banks, Digital Asset Curator and Archivist
Susan Roitman, Office Manager (Toronto)
Mary Mellas, Executive Assistant and Human Resources (Montreal)

Mark Goldstein, Art Director
François Blanc, Cartographer
Bruno Paradis, Layout, French-Language Editions

Contents

Series Preface: In their own words...

In telling these stories, the writers have liberated themselves. For so many years we did not speak about it, even when we became free people living in a free society. Now, when at last we are writing about what happened to us in this dark period of history, knowing that our stories will be read and live on, it is possible for us to feel truly free. These unique historical documents put a face on what was lost, and allow readers to grasp the enormity of what happened to six million Jews — one story at a time.

David J. Azrieli, C.M., C.Q., M.Arch
Holocaust survivor and founder, The Azrieli Foundation

Since the end of World War II, approximately 40,000 Jewish Holocaust survivors have immigrated to Canada. Who they are, where they came from, what they experienced and how they built new lives for themselves and their families are important parts of our Canadian heritage. The Azrieli Foundation's Holocaust Survivor Memoirs Program was established in 2005 to preserve and share the memoirs written by those who survived the twentieth-century Nazi genocide of the Jews of Europe and later made their way to Canada. The program is guided by the conviction that each survivor of the Holocaust has a remarkable story to tell, and that such stories play an important role in education about tolerance and diversity.

Millions of individual stories are lost to us forever. By preserving the stories written by survivors and making them widely available to a broad audience, the Azrieli Foundation's Holocaust Survivor Memoirs Program seeks to sustain the memory of all those who perished at the hands of hatred, abetted by indifference and apathy. The personal accounts of those who survived against all odds are as different as the people who wrote them, but all demonstrate the courage, strength, wit and luck that it took to prevail and survive in such terrible adversity. The memoirs are also moving tributes to people — strangers and friends — who risked their lives to help others, and who, through acts of kindness and decency in the darkest of moments, frequently helped the persecuted maintain faith in humanity and courage to endure. These accounts offer inspiration to all, as does the survivors' desire to share their experiences so that new generations can learn from them.

The Holocaust Survivor Memoirs Program collects, archives and publishes select survivor memoirs and makes the print editions available free of charge to educational institutions and Holocaust-education programs across Canada. They are also available for sale to the general public at bookstores. All revenues to the Azrieli Foundation from the sales of the Azrieli Series of Holocaust Survivor Memoirs go toward the publishing and educational work of the memoirs program.

~

The Azrieli Foundation would like to express appreciation to the following people for their invaluable efforts in producing this book: Doris Bergen, Sherry Dodson (Maracle Inc), Dana Francoeur, Farla Klaiman, Malcolm Lester, Therese Parent, and Margie Wolfe & Emma Rodgers of Second Story Press.

About the Glossary

The following memoir contains a number of terms, concepts and historical references that may be unfamiliar to the reader. For information on major organizations; significant historical events and people; geographical locations; religious and cultural terms; and foreign-language words and expressions that will help give context and background to the events described in the text, please see the glossary beginning on page 127.

Introduction

Tibor Benyovits was twelve years old when Budapest turned into a "Holocaust City."[1] It was 1944, the last full year of World War II, and the last chapter in the mass killings of European Jewry had started.[2] In one year, Tibor experienced more trauma than any child should ever have to. As a direct effect of the anti-Jewish laws and the war in Hungary, Tibor and his friends' education collapsed. He lost his home, lived apart from his family for several months, experienced heavy bombings, witnessed fellow-citizens being severely injured and saw piles of corpses, and suffered from severe illness and malnutrition. As Tibor expresses it, his childhood ended there and then — and it did so very abruptly.

In late 1944, Tibor's two older brothers were killed, and in January 1945, his father was shot to death by the Nyilas (the Hungarian fascist Arrow Cross Party). The Benyovits family, like many of the Jewish families in Budapest in 1944–1945, was truncated, and those who remained were scattered for years and decades in distant places. No child should encounter these things, but Tibor did, and like other survivors, his wartime experiences overshadowed his future life in many ways.

---

1   Tim Cole, *Holocaust City: The Making of a Jewish Ghetto* (New York: Routledge, 2003).

2   Götz Aly and Christian Gerlach, *Das letzte Kapitel: Realpolitik, Ideologie und der Mord an den ungarischen Juden 1944–1945* (Stuttgart and München: Deutsche Verlags-Anstalt, 2002).

Tibor was the youngest of five children in the Benyovits family. His father, David, was the general manager at the Reform Bethlen Square Synagogue, and they lived in an apartment close to the synagogue. Tibor describes his father as an upright, law-abiding person, an Orthodox Jew in his early fifties. His mother, Helen, was, according to Tibor, a sensitive and sympathetic person, the centre of the family. She cooked delicious meals and was a great hostess. The family often had lunch and dinner guests; Tibor remembers the Friday nights of his childhood as delightful, with much conversation and singing around the dinner table. His extended family played an important role in his life, especially his Aunt Elza, a younger sister of Tibor's mother who lived with the family during his childhood years. Eleven years younger than his eldest brother, Jenö, Tibor looked up to his older siblings, whom he describes as confident and fearless, especially Edith, who was eight years older than Tibor. Edith has an active role in Tibor's story, and even more so in the history of Hungarian Jews. A clever young woman, she saved the lives of her siblings and other Jews in Budapest on several occasions through networking, getting information, fixing false certificates and finding a job or a place to stay for people in need. She is one of those people to whom Tibor dedicates his memoirs — the "unsung heroes," as he calls them — the Zionist youth who saved countless numbers of lives through underground activities in Budapest and throughout Europe during the Holocaust.

Tibor joined Hanhac (Hanoar Hatzioni), a Zionist youth organization, at the age of eight. He enjoyed the activities and the community, new friends and the common dream of aliyah — the hope of immigrating to the Land of Israel and being part of building the country. This dream runs through Tibor's story, and it becomes obvious to the reader that it was a driving force in his life, especially during the war and the years after it.

The Holocaust in Hungary has been called the last chapter in

the annihilation of European Jewry.[3] Even though Jewish economic
and social life had been restricted by a number of anti-Jewish laws,
and there was considerable antisemitism in Hungarian society, there
had been very few systematic mass killings like those in Poland and
elsewhere in Eastern Europe during the first years of war. Hungarian Jewry was relatively safe until Germany occupied Hungary in
March 1944. Just a few months later, in May, the first deportations
of the Hungarian Jews went to Auschwitz-Birkenau. The cogwheels
of the destruction machinery were by this time running smoothly
and effectively: within two months, the Hungarian countryside was
basically emptied of Jews, except for the Jews of Budapest and Jewish
males in the labour force.

Before the war, the Hungarian Jewish population numbered approximately 800,000. Under the direction of Nazi leader Adolf Eichmann, the Germans, in cooperation with the Hungarian authorities,
deported about 434,000 individuals during the summer of 1944.
Most of them were gassed to death in Auschwitz-Birkenau.[4] Tibor's
relatives living in a town north of Budapest were deported, and only
a few of them survived. In July, the Hungarian regent Miklós Horthy
halted the deportations, and in this way he secured the survival of
Jews living in Budapest, at least for a few more months. Eichmann
tried to stage new deportations in late August, but this time the neutral countries protested.[5]

The ghettoization of Budapest Jewry was planned during the summer, but the actual ghetto in the Jewish quarter of Pest was not created
until November 1944. In the meantime, so-called Jewish houses were
established in apartment buildings all over the city.[6] In June 1944,
Tibor, together with his brother Jozsef and his parents, were ordered

3 Referring to Aly and Gerlach's book title, *Das letzte Kapitel*.
4 Randolph L. Braham, *The Politics of Genocide: The Holocaust in Hungary*, 2 vols. (New York: Columbia University Press, 1994), 674; Aly and Gerlach, *Das letzte Kapitel*.
5 Braham, *Politics of Genocide*, vol. 2, 915–919.
6 Cole, *Holocaust City*, chap. 7.

to move into a Jewish house on Király Street. They shared a small apartment with two other families, but still, they had a "home" where they could stay together. Tibor's older sisters, Magda and Edith, had moved out, and lived under false Christian identities elsewhere in the city. His brother Jenö had been drafted into the forced labour service in 1942 but came back to Budapest on furlough in 1944. Tibor describes how their freedom was regulated by a curfew and how, after some time, they were not allowed to go out at all. However, Tibor continued sneaking out without his yellow star to get supplies for his family.

On October 15, 1944, the Hungarian fascist Arrow Cross Party seized power. Persecution of Jews started immediately after the takeover, and the remaining months of the war were characterized by random violence and killings of Jewish inhabitants around the city. Arrow Cross men and Hungarian police raided Jewish houses, shot people into the Danube River or forced them to the brickyards of Óbuda, where they were taken on to the Austrian border or sent to forced labour service.[7] After the Nyilas takeover, the lives of the Benyovits family members also changed drastically. One day in late October, a man in disguise came to the Jewish house to fetch Tibor and take him to a villa on Orsó Street that belonged to Hanhac, the Zionist group. In the meantime, Tibor's father, David, fifty-two years old at that time, and his sixteen-year-old brother, Jozsef, were taken to the forced labour units. A few days later, Jenö was also taken away, and their mother, Helen, was left alone in the Jewish house.

The labour service system had a drastic impact on the Benyovits family. From 1939 onwards, Jewish males of military age, from twenty to forty-eight, were called up for forced labour, and the number of draftees increased significantly as Hungary joined the war in June 1941. In 1942, approximately 100,000 Jewish men served in the labour

---

7 Braham, *Politics of Genocide*, vol. 2.

service in the Hungarian army. The workers were not given the right to bear arms, and the work was physically strenuous. The brutality of these work units increased throughout the war, and the labour service men suffered from malnutrition, diseases and assaults, alongside warfare and extreme weather. Ironically, by the end of the war, many Jewish men could thank the labour service for their survival, since they simply were not at home at the time of the deportations. Even though thousands of Jewish males were killed in the labour forces, the survival rate was higher than for those who were deported.[8]

Directly after the Arrow Cross takeover in October 1944, the labour service was extended to all Jewish males between sixteen and sixty years, as well as Jewish females between eighteen and forty years of age. This is when Tibor's brother Jozsef and their father, David, were taken away to the labour battalions.

Fleeing from forced labour was punishable by death, and both Edith and Jozsef took a great risk when she rescued her little brother from the labour service. Somehow, Edith managed to get in contact with her brother and father and helped arrange for Jozsef to run away from the marching battalion. She then helped him obtain false Christian identity papers and get a job. During the last months of his life, Jozsef was living undercover in Budapest, working at a printing company that supplied material to the Hungarian defense department. Edith also tried to rescue their father, but David refused; as the law-abiding citizen that he was, he preferred to go through official channels. David was killed in the labour service in January 1945, after his unit was transferred to the Austrian border.

During this time, Tibor worked for the Hanhac organization. He functioned as a courier, carrying documents (i.e., safety passports or false identity papers) and supplies to various hiding places. He became street-smart, learning how to "act gentile," and to anticipate

---

8   Braham, *Politics of Genocide*, chap. 10.

and navigate obstacles and risky situations in the streets. This was extremely dangerous, since Jewish males could be revealed at any time through so-called "trouser inspections,"[9] which would determine if a male was circumcised, a ritual practiced only by Jews at that time. Tibor's young age was a possible advantage; nobody suspected a twelve-year-old child of being a courier for an underground movement. In any case, a person had to have a certain amount of courage and self-confidence to be able to handle a role like this. Showing no fear was a survival strategy for Tibor and the other Zionist resisters. Many comrades were lost in these trouser inspections, but as Tibor expresses it, "For our girls, it was a little bit easier" (p. 31) to move around the city. Gender mattered, as did age, for the Jewish experience in Budapest.

Tibor also mentions the different types of uniforms and disguises that the Hanhac members wore: Red Cross, Nyilas, Hungarian army, SS and police uniforms all enabled more freedom of movement and the ability to carry out resistance activities. According to Tibor, the Hanhac resisters wore mainly Arrow Cross and German SS uniforms. Without these uniforms, male individuals were not able to move freely around the city, as all adult males were supposed to be in the labour service or in the army. This is something that many Jewish and non-Jewish eyewitnesses have noted in their memoirs and interviews.[10] Another noteworthy detail that Tibor mentions is that no guns were used by Hanhac members because it was too dangerous. Tibor recalls one incident when one of his Hanhac comrades defied this rule and was killed when he was discovered carrying weapons on a streetcar.

The Zionist underground movement in Hungary consisted of several factions that operated throughout the war. But as Randolph Braham writes, most of the resistance and rescue activities by the Zi-

---

9 Laura Palosuo, *Yellow Stars and Trouser Inspections: Jewish Testimonies from Hungary, 1920–1945* (Uppsala, Sweden: Uppsala University, 2008).

10 Palosuo, *Yellow Stars*, 205-217; Robert Rozett, "Jewish Armed Resistance in Hungary: A Comparative View," in *Genocide and Rescue: The Holocaust in Hungary 1944*, ed. David Cesarani (Mid Clamorgan, UK: W B C Book Manufacturers, 1997).

onist groups were conducted during the Nyilas era in late 1944 and early 1945. In Budapest, the activists produced and distributed large numbers of false documents, including "Aryan" identification papers, safety passports and even SS and Nyilas membership cards. Individuals in Zionist resistance groups also rescued Jews from immediate danger in the streets and fed thousands of children living across the city. It is impossible to estimate how many lives the Zionist resistance groups, such as Tibor's Hanhac, actually saved. By the end of the war, about 130,000 Jews remained in Budapest, from a total of 230,000 before the war.[11]

Scholar Robert Rozett has shown that Jewish armed resistance in Hungary and in Budapest was very rare. There were several reasons for this, but mainly it was due to the fact that most of the Jewish men of "fighting age" had been drafted into the labour service. Furthermore, the German occupation occurred rather late in the war, and there was simply no time to organize armed resistance. According to Rozett, the Hungarian Jewish resistance consisted mainly of diplomatic (or bureaucratic) resistance, escape abroad and the manufacturing and spreading of false documents.[12] Tibor's mother was one of those saved by the false documents made by the Hanhac activists. Helen ended up in the Budapest ghetto, where conditions were extremely poor and the residents' fate uncertain. A new set of identity papers was created, and a German Jew who had joined the SS managed to get her out.

Sweden, Switzerland and the Vatican intervened through bureaucratic resistance and created an "international ghetto" with protected buildings north of the city centre of Pest. The inhabitants of these buildings received safety passports from the neutral countries, which would protect them from deportation or from the labour force.[13]

---

11 Braham, *Politics of Genocide,* 185; see also Asher Cohen, *The Halutz Resistance in Hungary 1942–1944* (New York: Columbia University Press, 1986).

12 Rozett, "Jewish Armed Resistance," 136–137, 142.

13 Cole, *Holocaust City*; see also Paul A. Levine, *From Indifference to Activism: Swedish Diplomacy and the Holocaust 1938–44* (Sweden: Uppsala University, 1998).

After being rescued from the ghetto, Helen was taken to her sister (who was living under a false Christian identity), but since the neighbours were suspicious, she was transferred to one of the protected buildings, where she lived until liberation in late January 1945. This building happened to be the synagogue where Tibor's father had been working.

It is interesting to look at how different factors affected the fate of Tibor's family members, and to see their experiences in a wider context of human experiences during the Holocaust. Geography, age and gender are perhaps the most easily identified as having influenced their fates.[14] First, geography: the Benyovits family lived in Budapest, and due to the halting of the deportations, their chances for survival were far greater than those of their relatives living outside Budapest. However, only the female members of the family and the youngest son, Tibor, survived. This leads us to the fact that age, intersecting gender, also mattered. Tibor was not drafted to the labour service — which both paradoxically saved some men and killed others — since he was only twelve in 1944. His eldest brother, Jenö, at twenty-seven, was killed by the Nyilas in Budapest in October 1944. Tibor's brother Jozsef had just turned sixteen when the age limit for the labour service was lowered. Although he escaped a labour force battalion, he died in a random shooting in the street in December 1944. Tibor's father, David, was also drafted into the labour service due to the new upper age limits, and was killed there. The female members of the family survived, it would seem, not merely because of their gender, but also because they took certain measures. Edith and Magda took their chances to live undercover as Christians, which kept them alive. Tibor's mother ended up in the ghetto, but was saved by Zionist resisters because of the intervention of Tibor and Edith.

---

14 This kind of analysis has been done by Cole in *Holocaust City* and by Palosuo in *Yellow Stars*.

What caused these young Zionists to undertake these heroic actions — creating false documents, wearing uniforms of disguise, moving people to safer places in the city and, in this way, risking their own lives? I do not have a conclusive answer, but I believe that schooling and the culture where they were raised did influence their actions in a crisis. Tibor and Edith were engaged with Hanhac at early ages; they had a common dream and a community they could depend on. Besides courage, the support that was apparently present in the Zionist organization of Hanhac must have increased one's chances of survival. This child, Tibor, and this young adult, Edith, had already experienced the strength of a group, and they knew that they could trust each other. Maybe this had something to do with their survival.

Tibor continued acting as a courier for the Hanhac organization until he was injured in an Arrow Cross raid, probably in early December 1944. His Hanhac group transported him to the Bethlen Synagogue, where he could stay with his mother. Tibor was in great pain. He writes: "This turn of events effectively finished my underground activities." (p. 46) Luckily there were doctors in the building, and with their help, Tibor eventually recovered. It took some time though, since he was undernourished and there was a constant lack of water.

For about forty days, Tibor and his mother lived in the Bethlen Synagogue, together with hundreds of other people. On January 20, 1945, the building was liberated by a Ukrainian unit within the Soviet army. The irony of the liberation is clear in Tibor's story: The officer who entered the building warned the people there not to tell anybody that they were Jewish, since his unit was very antisemitic. Tibor describes this moment as a cold shower.

After the end of the Siege of Budapest, they still lacked food and water, but now they could move around the adjacent blocks and try to find some supplies. Tibor and Helen were able to move back to their old apartment, and things started to slowly get better. In March, they received the devastating news about Tibor's father, and gradu-

ally they also heard the news about their extended family. Tibor's uncles and aunts on his mother's side had survived, but his grandparents
and most of his cousins were murdered.

In late spring of 1945, Tibor got in contact with Hanhac again
through an older cousin on his father's side, Yehuda Benyovits. Yehuda suggested that Tibor join a group of 120 children that would leave
Hungary for Germany and from there go on to Israel. Tibor's mother
wasn't too excited at this prospect, but in the end, they decided that
Tibor would leave, in hope of finding a better future. The journey to
Israel started in January 1946 and was rather complicated. The group
was stuck in Aschau, Germany, for months. In December 1946, Tibor
and two of his friends were tired of waiting, and they decided to go
back to Budapest.

In 1948, Israel was declared an independent state. Tibor still
dreamed of aliyah, hoping to escape the harshness of the new communist regime in Hungary, which did not allow for religious or Zionist identity. In April 1949, he and some of his group managed to
escape from Hungary to Czechoslovakia, Austria and Italy. In July,
the ship named "Independence" departed the port of Bari in Italy
and took them to Haifa. Tibor remembers his feelings about leaving
Europe: he didn't feel too much regret since the loss of his father, two
brothers and other family members had made him bitter and angry
at his former countrymen. Hungary had let them down, and Tibor
felt no desire to stay.

Upon their arrival in Israel, Tibor was placed in a *mossad*, a youth
institution close to the kibbutz Tel Yitzhak. During the first year in
his new homeland, he went to school and helped with the harvest at
the kibbutz. Tibor sang in the *mossad* choir and tried to adjust to his
new life. Tibor met his future wife, Miriam, in the army, and they
married in 1953 and soon started a family. Tibor describes the 1950s
as a period in his life when most of his dreams were fulfilled. But
something was missing — "the devil started to work on me and I ended up doing something I never thought I would" (p. 114). Miriam and

Tibor started to plan to move to Canada in order to earn some money so that he could save up to start his own machine shop in Israel. By that time, Tibor's sister Edith was living in Canada with her family, as was Tibor's mother. In Canada, everything seemed possible. So in 1962, after a few years of planning, they moved to Toronto. After many years of hard work, Tibor (who now went by Ted) was able to start his own business, but the family never returned to live in Israel.

Tibor Benyovits' testimony is an important contribution to the relatively unknown history of Zionist resistance in Budapest and to the Holocaust in Hungary. He dedicates his memoir to the "unsung heroes" he knew in the Hanhac organization, but I am not sure if he realizes that he himself is one of these unknown heroes. Without him and all the other youngsters who risked their lives in the streets of Budapest, many more Jewish lives would have been lost. For me, Tibor, the twelve-year-old courier, and Edith, the courageous young woman who saved her brother from the labour service and her mother from the ghetto, symbolize faith. Their actions remind us that even in a crisis, with very little hope, one individual can still make a difference. Tibor's story gives us hope in decency and humanity. Joining forces matters to all of us.

Laura Brander (formerly Palosuo)
PhD History
Educational developer at Mid Sweden University
2018

REFERENCES AND FURTHER READINGS

Aly, Götz and Christian Gerlach. *Das letzte Kapitel. Realpolitik, Ideologie und der Mord an den ungarischen Juden 1944–1945.* Stuttgart & München: Deutsche Verlags-Anstalt, 2002.

Braham, Randolph L. *The Politics of Genocide: The Holocaust in Hungary.* 2 vols. New York: Columbia University Press, 1994.

Braham, Randolph L. "Rescue Operations in Hungary: Myths and Realities." *East European Quarterly* 38, no. 2 (Summer 2004): 173(31).

Cohen, Asher. *The Halutz Resistance in Hungary 1942–1944*. New York: Columbia University Press, 1986.

Cole, Tim. *Holocaust City: The Making of a Jewish Ghetto*. New York: Routledge, 2003.

Genizi, Haim and Naomi Blank, "The Rescue Efforts of Bnei Akiva in Hungary During the Holocaust." *Yad Vashem Studies* 23 (1993):173–212.

Kramer, Tom D. *From Emancipation to Catastrophe: The Rise and Holocaust of Hungarian Jewry*. Lanham, USA: University Press of America, 2000.

Levine, Paul A. *From Indifference to Activism: Swedish Diplomacy and the Holocaust 1938–44*. Uppsala, Sweden: Uppsala University, 1998.

Palosuo, Laura. *Yellow Stars and Trouser Inspections: Jewish Testimonies from Hungary, 1920–1945*. Uppsala, Sweden: Uppsala University, 2008.

Rozett, Robert, "Jewish Armed Resistance in Hungary: A Comparative View." *Genocide and Rescue: The Holocaust in Hungary 1944*. Edited by David Cesarani. Mid Clamorgan, UK: WBC Book Manufacturers, 1997.

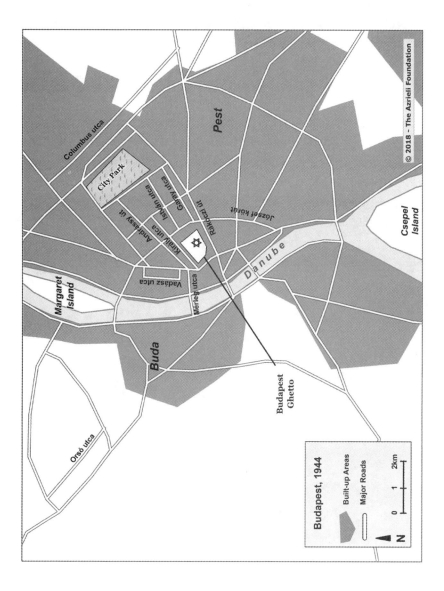

Budapest, 1944

Built-up Areas
Major Roads

0   1   2km

N

Margaret Island

Orsó utca

Buda

Columbus utca

City Park

Andrássy út

Király utca

István utca

Gábor utca

Vadász utca

Mérleg utca

Rákóczi út

József körút

Pest

Danube

Csepel Island

Budapest Ghetto

© 2018 – The Azrieli Foundation

Author's Preface

The purpose of my book is to put a face on the forgotten or ignored activities of the Zionist youth in Hungary during the worst period of 1944. Their underground activities were instrumental in saving untold numbers of lives. With totally selfless dedication, in danger every minute, instead of lying low with their false papers in hiding places supplied by their Zionist leadership, they went out to help thousands of needy Jews who were in protected houses outside of the Budapest ghetto.[1] This took place when the war was almost over and Soviet forces had surrounded Budapest.

To my knowledge, no specific literature exists about this group of youngsters and their heroic exploits. In my opinion, Jewish historians have neglected or discounted heroic actions unless the individuals or groups were fighting with weapons.[2] In Budapest, the goal of the

---

1   For information on the Budapest ghetto as well as on other historical, religious and cultural terms; significant historical events and people; geographical locations; major organizations; and foreign-language words and expressions contained in the text, please see the glossary.

2   There are some Hebrew and Hungarian sources on the work of Zionist youth organizations in Hungary during the war. One English-language source is David Gur's *Brothers for Resistance and Rescue: The Underground Zionist Youth Movement in Hungary During World War II*. (Jerusalem: The Society for the Research of the History of the Zionist Youth Movement in Hungary, 2009.)

underground groups was to save as many lives as possible as the war drew to a close. Each of the Zionist groups had or could have had weapons and used them to kill a few Nazis. But in the process, many Jews might not have been saved.

During the more than five years of World War II, there were groups of partisans or other fighters who succeeded in killing a great number of the enemy. But I don't believe that these deaths reduced the millions of Jewish victims of the Nazi killing machine. Our Zionist underground groups, on the other hand, had the privilege of effectively saving the last remnant of Jews in Europe, sometimes with the help of foreign diplomats like Raoul Wallenberg and Carl Lutz. To me, the actions of the Zionist youth during those dark times represent the ultimate in heroism and sacrifice.

This book is dedicated to these unknown heroes, living and dead.

A Community of Family

As far back as I can remember, my close family consisted of my father, David; my mother, Helen; my five siblings; and the unmarried youngest sister of my mother, my aunt Elza. We all lived together in a tiny two-bedroom apartment. My eldest brother was Jenö, born in 1921; then came my eldest sister, Magda, in 1922; after her, Edith was born in 1924; my brother Jozsef, who was also called Suci, was born in 1927; and finally I, the baby of the family, called Tibou or Tibi, was born in 1932. We lived on the second floor at 23 Garay utca, street, in Budapest, one block away from the busy eastern railway station.

Looking back, it is hard to believe that we all managed to live together in such a small place. In addition to the eight of us, we often had relatives coming to Budapest and staying with us while doing their weekly shopping for their small businesses. These relatives, the brothers and sisters of my mother, lived in outlying towns and took the train to the eastern railway station. Even with this overcrowdedness, we were a very happy family.

My siblings and I went to various Jewish schools, all of which started at and ended at different times. This created a huge challenge for my mother when planning to cook meals, a challenge that she handled with aplomb. On top of the eight of us, and sometimes our relatives, an old gentleman we called Uncle Jenö ate his lunch and dinner with us. Uncle Jenö, who worked for my father, had no family, so at mealtime he became part of ours. His hygiene wasn't good and we kids didn't enjoy being with him, but our parents felt it was their duty to look after him, so we weren't allowed to voice any objections.

My dear mother, whom I feel should have received the designation of "saint" for all her jobs and duties, still found the time to teach us many kinds of songs — songs from World War I, popular songs of the time and arias of operettas and operas. As a child, I was put to sleep with an aria from *The Tales of Hoffmann*. Our whole family loved singing — from traditional Jewish melodies to operas. Most of these songs from my childhood are still fresh in my memory sixty-five years later.

My father was the *főnök*, general manager, of a fair-sized synagogue called the Bethlen tér, square, Synagogue. Working under him were four *shamashim*, assistants, two for the women's floor and two for the men's, or sanctuary, floor. The synagogue had two rabbis, one cantor and a choirmaster. The Bethlen tér was a Neolog, or Reform synagogue, and served hundreds of families in the neighbourhood. It was a sizable complex that included, besides the synagogue, a Jewish elementary school and kindergarten, an extensive sports facility with a fully equipped gym, basketball and tennis courts, a soccer field and an extensive office section for the congregation.

As soon as World War II began in September 1939, the Bethlen complex housed the National Bureau of the Jews of Hungary, also known as OMZSA, which assisted those who needed help. First were Jewish refugees from Austria, Czechoslovakia and other German-occupied countries. My dear father, with his great heart, always found some refugee couple with or without children and would bring them home on Fridays for Shabbat dinners. There was no telephone with which to warn my mother that there would be additional mouths to feed. At any rate, no one ever left our table hungry.

Then, starting in 1939, when Hungarian Jewish youth were conscripted into forced-labour battalions, an offshoot organization of the Bureau provided clothing, food and other necessities — socks, shawls, gloves — which the organization's women collected or made themselves. In short, the Bethlen complex was a very busy place. In 1939, the Hungarian Jewish community numbered over 800,000 and the Neolog community, to which 65 per cent of Jews belonged, had a specific structure.[3] Actually, it was almost a country in itself. Jewish Neolog institutions like synagogues, schools, hospitals, old-age homes, cemeteries and even Jewish sport organizations all belonged to the National Bureau of the Jews of Hungary. Each employee of a Jewish institution was paid by the national organization, and to cover these extensive costs, a special tax was levied on the Jewish community. The tax was implemented through the different synagogues Jews belonged to, and the collection of these taxes was the job of the synagogue for each particular district.

The job of collection in our synagogue was my father's, and he had to carry it out mostly on foot. No car or phone was available. The work required constant walking and, in many cases, climbing lots of stairs in buildings without elevators. Often the person who was supposed to pay the tax was not home or had no money at the time of the visit, so it was a very hard and heart-rending job. My father, exhausted, usually fell asleep after dinner. Still, he participated in our Sunday outings to the Buda Mountains, where the family played and picnicked when I was young.

Our whole life revolved around my father's synagogue, and I spent most of my day-to-day hours there. The daily prayers, as well as my kindergarten and elementary school, were concentrated in the

---

3 In 1868, a General Jewish Congress was called to attempt to unify the Jewish community under one overarching internal structure. However, the communities remained divided; alongside the larger Neolog community was the Orthodox community (comprising 29 per cent of Jews), whose national organization was called the Central Bureau of the Autonomous Orthodox Jewish Community. The Status Quo Ante community, which was the smallest, at 5 per cent, was independent and had no national organization.

Bethlen complex. In the same complex, there was a large apartment for the secretary general of the National Bureau. His position was almost as important as a Hungarian parliamentarian's. On certain occasions when he went to visit high-ranking government officials, he even had a police escort. He had a large, chauffeur-driven car and was a respected official. The secretary general controlled almost anything that was connected with the Hungarian Neolog congregation, which numbered approximately 500,000. He and his wife had three kids, two of whom were not much older than me. We were friends and met quite often on Saturdays when we could use facilities that were out of reach for others — because of our privileged status, we could get the keys for places that were closed on Shabbat, the Sabbath.

We especially liked to play in the gym room. The well-equipped gym had a sawdust floor and was full of wooden or leather structures — jump horses, swings and ropes with rings — for climbing and other exercises. The gym had a large collection of balls as well as a hoop for basketballs. It was a lot of fun, especially because we alone could use all the facilities, which otherwise would have been available to us only in our regular classes.

Later on Saturday afternoons, my father would come back to one of the synagogue's offices to prepare the customary third meal of the Sabbath. He would have the shopping done on Friday for this event: drinks, breads or buns and a wide variety of cold cuts — my favourite — and fruits. The leftover cold cuts served us well for the usual family Sunday picnic trips to the Mountains of Buda. Older members of the synagogue usually attended this third meal and one of the congregants donated money for the cost of it, either in honour of upcoming weddings and bar mitzvahs or in remembrance of departed family members. I had a special function in the Saturday evening service after the third meal. I sang a prayer at this time and it gave me great satisfaction to see the congregants enjoy my song.

At home, the Friday night dinners, the Saturday lunches and the holiday meals had significance besides the delicious food my mother served us. These were the times when we sang beautiful songs, in which the whole family participated. If we didn't have special guests, we often invited female friends of the family to enjoy the food and the meaningful atmosphere of prayer and song. Two were our next-door neighbours, Aunt Manci and Daty. Daty was like part of our family. She and her artist husband had been our neighbours at the previous apartment our family had lived in.

Daty had no children and treated my brother Jozsef (Suci) and my sister Edith as her own. She had very little family in general and we filled this void. When we moved to the Garay utca apartment, she started visiting us for Friday dinners, which she enjoyed very much. When we had lived next door to her, she spent a lot of Friday dinners with us and learned most of the Friday night songs, joining in when we sang. She stayed close to us even when things started to get rough for Jews in Budapest. She visited us anytime we had to move, and she brought us supplies we couldn't get anymore. And when our situation worsened, we gave her a few valuable items and pictures for safekeeping. She lived in a distant suburb called Zugló. In good times before the occupation, if we didn't see her for a few Fridays, we would go to visit her by streetcar.

I was also quite close with Aunt Manci, a middle-aged woman living alone with a dog. I accompanied her when she went shopping or on walks with her dog. A few times, she took me to her church. She also was a frequent guest in our apartment, spending many Saturdays or holidays with us at our table. As an Orthodox family, we had some restrictions on our behaviour at these times. For example, we were prohibited from starting or extinguishing lights or fires on Shabbat. She became our Shabbat helper, turning off the lights and the oven. I didn't realize at the time how well such neighbourly contacts — and, through them, my familiarity with gentile customs — would serve me in later tragic times.

In the city, we kids learned a lot of street smarts. The surrounding streets were the only place to play after school and homework. We went to the flea market, a substantial distance from home, and with a few cents in our pockets, we purchased ball bearings and two bars with treads to build our own scooters. The bearings and bars served as the base, and we found some wood for the platform and the upright parts. When our creations were ready, we had a lot of fun with them. Our street was made of cobblestones but the next street and the sidewalks were made of asphalt, which was a perfect place for competitions and games. We also made balls from discarded socks, which were later replaced by real rubber balls, just as the scooters were eventually replaced by bicycles.

In 1940, when I joined the Zionist group Hanoar Hatzioni (The Zionist Youth), which we called Hanhac for short, I had to get around the city for the mid-week meetings, which was complicated and costly by regular transportation; in addition, many of the group members lived in locations that streetcar lines didn't reach. But getting a bicycle wasn't an easy task because my father was not wealthy. So we made a deal that I would look for a used bicycle, and the money would come partially from him and the rest from my savings. I had a few sources — partly in our synagogue, partly from visiting relatives and for services rendered to the super or our next-door neighbour, Aunt Manci, for bringing cigarettes or doing other shopping.

All of my cousins were heavily involved in the Zionist movement, mostly as members of Hanoar Hatzioni. Their house was a real meeting place, and I got acquainted with many of the boys and girls in the group there. I liked the songs and the lectures as well as the members. Although at the time I was only eight years old, I felt that I wanted to belong to such a group that dreamt about the land the British then called Palestine but we called *Eretz Yisrael*, the Land of Israel.

They all wanted to become pioneers on kibbutzim, collective farms. Some of my cousins had already made aliyah, moved to the Land of Israel, so I started to nag those of my cousins who were leaders of the organization to let me join. The problem was that you had to be at least twelve years old. With persistence, finally, a way was found to allow me to join the organization. There were, of course, concerns about my maturity — the organization was already on a semi-underground footing because of the war and because Hungary had become a close ally of Germany. All our activities went under the name and cover of the Budapest Jewish Youth Cultural Organization.

Hanoar Hatzioni, along with other Zionist youth groups, was made up of *kvutzot*, small groups, of eight to twelve kids and one or two older leaders. All the *kvutzot* belonged to a *kein*, a nest. The *kvutzot* met once every week, rotating among members' apartments. Saturday was the meeting of the *kein*. This would be in a large hall that was officially recognized as a Jewish youth cultural centre, requiring membership and a yearly fee. Again, the same problem arose for me: you could be a member only if you were twelve or older. So every Saturday when we went to our *kein* meeting, a group of boys and girls created a distraction that allowed me to sneak in.

At the meetings, there were speeches about the variety of problems Jews were now facing in different countries and locales. It was very depressing. On top of this were the reports on the status of the Jews of Hungary — the gradual restrictions on employment, on higher education, on the conduct of business and so on. As the war continued and the restrictions became more severe, we began to prepare for the time when things would be unmanageable: when we would be required to move totally underground equipped with false identity papers, secure hiding places, alternative supply routes and safe forms of communication.

Meanwhile, those Saturday meetings also had their social side when we would sing, dance, meet with our favourite friends and talk about the third of the weekly gatherings of our *kvutzot*, the customary Sunday trip to the Buda Mountains. This was the activity we all loved most. Our routine was to meet every Sunday at the same location, beside the western railway station. The intersection of two major streets created four islands. One was called the "banana" island as in the past it had been a banana market. This island had a giant clock under which we would meet in the summertime at 6:00 a.m. and in the wintertime at 7:00 a.m. The day's program was never disclosed in advance, and the group waited for only five minutes before departing. We loved those outings so very much that everyone made an extra effort to be on time. Since I lived on the other side of the city, I took an early streetcar that sometimes delivered me to the meeting point way ahead of the appointed hour.

If the weather was rainy, instead of the mountain trip we would go to the Margaret Island swimming complex. It had three pools inside and three outside and both functioned year-round. In winter, we would run outside on the snowy decks and jump into the heated pool, which was covered with a cloud because the water from the pool evaporated in the cold air. When we finished our outside swim, we would swim via a tunnel to the inside part of the complex. This pool was the training pool for all the top swimmers right up to the Olympic-class swimmers.

In the *kvutzah*, small group, there were boys and girls. We each brought our own supply of sandwiches, fruits and sweet stuff. When it was time to have our snack or lunch, all our supplies were mixed together, and then the girls usually set out the meal. This way, no one needed to feel badly because his or her parents could afford only a simple food package.

When I was about ten years old, I had my first girlfriend in our group. Her name was Shoshanah and she had a beautiful face and smile. Our relationship didn't last too long because she stopped coming to our meetings, and I couldn't find out what became of her.

⁓

In late 1943, our Hanhac group got a special notification through the pre-arranged grapevine that had been set up for emergencies. The message called us for an unusual meeting on Friday instead of the customary Saturday one. The reason, as we found out later, was that a member of our Zionist youth organization from Poland had come to speak to us. He told us that he had been taken to a concentration camp where most of the prisoners ended up in the gas chamber. He and a few others were able to escape and he had taken it upon himself to warn the Jewish communities not yet occupied by the Germans to prepare the means and ways to save as many Jews as possible. As he spoke, the large meeting hall was in total darkness. Only at the head table were a few candles lit. Against this background, these gruesome stories shook us to the core.

Like most Hungarian Jews, we lived with the false hope that in Hungary those kinds of things would not happen. Sure, there were all kinds of restrictions and anti-Jewish laws, but the lives of the Jews were reasonably routine. The majority of Hungary's Jews had assimilated; thousands of Hungarian Jews had even converted to Christianity. Jews had fought with great distinction in World War I, achieving high ranks and exceptional honours. In short, Hungarian Jews were Hungarian patriots first, and Jews second.

According to what was later told to me, after our Polish visitor met with us and other Zionist organizations, the leaders of these organizations approached the heads of the Jewish communities to convey this news. They asked the heads to inform their communities so they would be able to devise some ways for survival. Their answer in effect was, "This won't happen here. If you spread this information to the people, we will disclose you to the authorities. Whatever happens, we will be able to handle it at the negotiating table." Given such a rebuff, the only thing that we could do was to prepare our organization for the extreme times to come.

In the meantime, we heard stories of our Jewish brothers' situation in the forced labour battalions. The system had been changing since first being implemented in 1939, and by 1941, all Jewish men from ages eighteen up to, I think, forty-two, were conscripted into these units. Depending on size, a military frame was created, although the units were unarmed. The head of the unit could be a colonel or major, but under him, all the Jews held no rank at all. The Hungarian army also didn't supply any equipment or clothing besides an army hat. This meant that the Jewish men had to bring everything they needed from home: clothing, shoes, winter stuff, cleaning, washing, shaving kits.

These battalions were attached to regular army units and travelled with them. The army units usually went by truck or train, while the Jews, most of the time, had to march after them. Their job was the hard work like fortifications, trench building, clearing of minefields and bombed buildings, and so on. The food supplied by the army was very meagre, so if some were lucky enough to have money, they could buy things to supplement their poor rations. How these units fared in these awful times mainly depended on the highest-ranking officer of the unit. If he was a decent fellow, he demanded the required tasks but treated the men as well as he could — luckily, this was my brother Jenö's experience when he was called up for the forced labour brigades in 1942. If, on the other hand, the officer was an antisemite, he could slowly finish the unit off. We heard horror stories about officers who punished the Jews for no reason, hanging them on trees with their hands behind their backs without touching the ground. Some officers not only hung them but also doused them with water during the winter. Certain punishments were so gruesome that their barbarity shouldn't be put down on paper.

To Move Freely

Although my father worked for a Neolog synagogue, he was an Orthodox individual. My father tried to instill the same religious commitment in his children. Although we all went to the elementary school of the Neolog synagogue, the plan for me and my brothers was to go to the *gimnázium*, high school, of the Orthodox stream. For me, it was a hard transition as most of my classmates from elementary school went directly to the Neolog junior high school, which had an excellent reputation. According to my father's wish and plan, I was to go to the Orthodox junior high for four years and then the Jewish high school, as my brother Suci had done.

The Orthodox school was located across the city from where we lived, and the school day had two parts; in the morning there was the regular school curriculum, and in the afternoon, the religious part of our studies. Around noon, we would go home for lunch. For most of the students from the Orthodox community, lunchtime presented no travel problem as they lived near the school. But the Neolog area where I lived required two trips back and forth daily to attend the morning and afternoon school sessions.

I travelled to my school by streetcar. The streetcar came from a faraway suburb and was usually full by the time it reached my stop. The only way to get on was to stand on the steps outside the car and hold on to the handle. Between stations, there was no relief for the hand clutching the handle. I prayed that I could hold on until the next station where I could change hands or relax the hand I was using to hang on, while the other hand held on to my school bag. In winter, my gloves would often freeze on the cold handle as I hung on for dear life.

Another problem for me was that in religious studies the Hebrew text was translated into Yiddish. Some Orthodox families used Yiddish at home, but this was not the case in our house. This made the study of Hebrew very difficult. And I had another stroke against me: I was a member of a Zionist organization and some considered Zionism to be the antithesis of the Jewish religion. The Orthodox believed that Israel could not be created arbitrarily by the Zionists but only by the coming of the Messiah. Therefore, the Orthodox community — including my school — forbade any participation in the Zionist movement and its activities. The school's authorities knew about our meeting places and they sent spies to see who from the school went to those Zionist meetings. And so, every Sunday morning, I would be called to the principal's office where Dr. Deutsch, the principal, would give me a serious lecture about the evils of Zionism, a speech that always included threats to expel me from school. Truth be told, I was praying for such a punishment, which I felt would save me from the school that I hated. In the end, a terrible event occurred that freed me from this predicament, an event for which I wouldn't have prayed had I known what was awaiting us Jews in Hungary. In fact, I had been in junior high only a little more than one and a half years when everything fell apart. On March 19, 1944, the most infamous day on the Hungarian Jewish calendar, the Germans occupied Hungary.

As luck would have it, my aunt Elza, my mother's youngest sister, who lived with us, was getting married to a man named Zoli that terrible day. The wedding was held at my grandparents' house in a small town called Vác, thirty-five kilometres from Budapest. All my aunts and uncles with their families came for the big event. That was the last time we saw most of them.

My grandfather's house was located on the main street of Vác. All day long there was a constant stream of German tanks, trucks with soldiers, large gun units, motorcycles. It seemed as though the whole German army was marching past. When we returned to Budapest from the wedding, people were being stopped in the railway station to have their papers checked. Many had already been detained by the police and soldiers. My sister Edith hadn't come to the wedding. She was engaged to the son of a famous gynecologist who had very powerful connections, and he'd had information about what would happen at the railway station and convinced her not to go. Luckily, our papers were not checked.

After this terrible day, things changed rapidly. New laws were proclaimed for the Jews, the most well-known being that Jews had to sew a yellow Star of David on their garments. Jews were also detained on all kinds of trumped-up charges; for example, if a Jew was reading a newspaper that covered the yellow star, he was grabbed and taken to an internment camp. Some were later released, but many were never heard from again.

In the outlying towns and villages, the Hungarian authorities moved quickly and eagerly to do the Germans' dirty work. Any order to be carried out was given to the Jewish leadership, who notified the Jews as to what they had to do. The Jews were told that they were going to be transferred to new accommodations to work for the war effort. They would be allowed to take only a small suitcase with the most essential items along with them and were given only a few hours to prepare for their evacuation.

Immediately after the occupation, the Hanhac group leaders met hurriedly. It was decided that members who came from outside Budapest would have the opportunity to go back to their families with false identity papers to try to smuggle them into Budapest, which seemed more secure for the time being. In very small villages or towns where everyone knew each other, this effort was dangerous. As soon as a new face appeared in town, even if it was someone's son or daughter who lived elsewhere, the local police were informed and the individual was arrested. If false papers were found, it often meant a tragic end to the individual and his or her family. In some instances, the parents didn't want to believe the son's or daughter's explanation as to why they should agree to their Zionist kids' crazy plans. Many of these parents, like most of the Hungarian Jewry, didn't believe the horrific stories of what was going to happen. Those who didn't have sufficient willpower to revolt against their parents' thinking stayed with them and died with them.

All levels of Jewish leadership had the same approach: cooperate with the authorities and negotiate with them to achieve the best outcome for their communities.

~

In mid-May, just two months after the occupation, the first deportations started. Police units called *csendőrs*, gendarmes, concentrated the Jews into smaller communities in the neighbouring towns. The Jews were then transported to a larger town that often had a brick factory. Brick factories were fenced off and usually beside railway lines. In these brick factories, the Jews were kept in terrible conditions. There were no washrooms, showers or other facilities. Food was scarce; the ones who brought some food with them could get by but the majority had nothing to eat, having calculated that wherever they would be taken food would be supplied.

As bad as these conditions were, they weren't the worst the Jews would face. Within about twelve weeks from the time of occupation, the Hungarians, in collaboration with the German authorities, deported approximately 440,000 Hungarian Jews to death camps in Poland. Considering that all this action was taking place when the war was almost lost and finished, you would think that the railways would be used for defensive purposes against the advancing enemy. The same reasoning can be applied to the very large amount of manpower that was required to execute this "Final Solution to the Jewish problem." What hatred the Hungarian police must have felt to execute these murderous actions with such zeal!

The stories that the few survivors of the deportations and the death camps told after the war were so horrific that it is hard for me to write of them. They told of how they had been so squeezed into the cattle wagons that they'd had to stand for lack of room. They told of the cattle wagons being sealed so tight that even the little windows had been covered and closed by wood or sheet metal so very little air could come in. They told of parents desperate to help their children, who suffered terribly from the lack of anything to drink. They told of people emptying their bowels and bladders, creating the worst stench any human could endure. They told of the violence and horror they had to withstand in order to survive the camps.

The war effort for the Axis forces — which included Germany, Hungary, Italy and Japan — went from bad to worse. All their armies were described by the news services as being "in tactical realignment," but we knew that meant they were retreating in panic. After the Battle of Stalingrad ended in February 1943, things had turned around for them and disasters instead of victories plagued their war effort. The little information we picked up from the "Voice of London" told us that the war had started to move toward the defeat of the Axis powers. As for the Jews of Europe, some of us understood that most were under the threat of death. But in 1944, Hungarian Jewish leaders still believed that, because Jews were Hungarian patriots — evidenced by the extremely large percentage of Jewish soldiers, relative to the Hungarian population, who had fought patriotically in World War I — we would be spared.

After the occupation began, we spent almost every night in the cellar, which was the safest place in times of aerial bombardment. The houses of long ago were built with extremely thick walls, and the cellars were divided into small cubicles belonging to each of the tenants.

The cubicles were used to store coal or wood for heating each apartment, or for other storage. When the bombing started, the apartment owners reorganized their cubicles to accommodate their family's needs for longer term stays in the cellar.

The apartment houses in Budapest were built with common areas in the form of a courtyard with four streets surrounding it. In each house, there was a way to connect through to the other. Instead of regular two- to three-feet-thick walls, just a layer of bricks was installed, which could be knocked over if the houses were bombed and the regular exits became blocked. This format, designed so tenants had alternate escape routes, saved a lot of lives. As Budapest was a very important industrial centre, the bombings concentrated on it a lot.

In the middle of Budapest runs the Duna (Danube) River, containing a number of islands. I mentioned one large island, Margaret, which stretches between two bridges. An even larger island named Csepel contains a huge industrial complex, the Csepel Works. This complex was owned and managed by a gentleman named Manfréd Weiss, who employed over forty thousand workers by the start of World War II. Csepel Works produced a wide variety of products — from locomotives to cannons and other weapons as well as tools, milling machines and drilling machines. They even produced bicycles and pots and pans. Most of Csepel's products were essential to the war effort. Knowing this, the Allies bombed Csepel Island relentlessly.

We spent more time in the bomb shelters than out of them. One day, the news claimed that the attacking force had included 1,200 bombers. They came in waves, each with a particular target area. The lead bomber would create a huge smoke circle and his wings only entered this ring and dropped the bombs. We called it carpet bombing. The devastation was unbelievable — the entire infrastructure of certain city districts was damaged or destroyed.

At night, large numbers of spotlights lit up the black skies, providing an amazing light show. If a spotlight succeeded at illuminating a plane, a second and third reflector immediately joined in, giving the anti-aircraft batteries a better chance to try to shoot it down. We prayed for the success of these attacks, which we hoped would bring the war to an end and our liberation closer.

The authorities passed the *statárium*, martial law, for which the penalty for transgression was death. At night, the city had to be totally dark. Even car lights had to be painted blue to limit their glow. On each window of a house, black curtains had to be installed. If a window was not completely closed and some light escaped, the minimum action that police or other protective units would take was to fire into the window. If the opening was larger, they could drag the violator to a court that had the power to hand down the death penalty. The authorities assumed that any such violation was espionage and that the perpetrator was signalling the enemy. Other violations punishable by death included rumour mongering; escaping from military services; spying in any form; and even listening to a transmission of enemy radio stations. The BBC's "Voice of London" was the best source for reliable information but listening to it was totally forbidden.

The bombing of Hungary was divided between the US and British air forces. The US, with their high-flying B-17 and liberator bombers, did the job during the day when anti-aircraft cannons couldn't touch them. The British, with their Lancaster and Halifax heavy bombers, did the night bombings. Tall buildings in the city of Budapest were equipped with and protected by multi-cannon aircraft guns.

Our house, as I mentioned, was one block away from the eastern railway station, and the gunners on our roof would start their salvos before we could even hear any aircraft noise. The information about a coming attack was also sent to everyone by radio. When it announced to the *bácska baja*, border towns, "Krokodil grosse" (big crocodiles), this was a code word in German that meant a large group of planes were crossing the border; the sirens would shriek, signalling the people of the city to get to the bomb shelters. We had five to ten minutes to get our bags to the cellar shelter before the noise of airplane motors could be heard overhead. Each house had a security warden who made sure everyone was accounted for, and I was one of the warden's helpers. The warden and his helpers were stationed outside the bomb shelter entrance. We rushed down when we felt that bombs were falling nearby. The house security warden also chose me to be his additional eyes and a courier if the need arose to contact other bordering houses in case of an emergency.

~

Our lives soon progressed from bad to worse. By June, there was a new law that differentiated between Jewish and gentile apartment houses, according to the number of Jewish tenants and gentile ones. Where Jews were a majority in the building, it was designated as a Jewish house, also called a yellow-star building. If they were not, then it stayed a gentile one, and the Jews were forced to move out. This happened to the four of us who remained at 23 Garay utca: my parents, Suci and I. My eldest sister, Magda, and youngest sister, Edith, had already been away for quite a while through the efforts of various underground organizations. According to the new regulations, we had to move to a different house across the city, where a distant relative provided us with one bedroom. Three families lived in this small apartment, sharing the kitchen and the facilities. We could take few things with us, as the room we got in the new apartment could not accommodate much. We had to leave virtually all our belongings in our vacated apartment, not knowing when or even if we could come back.

The apartment building, which had been designated a Jewish house, was a sizable one with two courtyards. It was located at 14 Király utca, King Street. In front was the well-known King Conditoria, a coffee shop, which was out of service when we moved in.

The Jews of Budapest, now concentrated in designated Jewish houses, were given new laws and regulations daily by a non-Jewish superintendent, whose job it was to carry out the prevailing anti-

Jewish regulations. At the outset, the curfew was strict and only allowed us to move around the city for three hours, from 2:00 p.m. to
5:00 p.m. The curfew regulations were posted inside Jewish houses
and outside on bulletin boards. Slowly, the curfew relaxed and the
time for free movement became longer — 11:00 a.m. to 5:00 p.m. But
suddenly, on one Thursday in October, our movement from the Jewish houses was shut down — no in and out anymore. Previously, I
would sneak out without the star to get supplies unavailable to us in
our allotted hours.

Long before the occupation, many food items — such as sugar,
flour, butter, jam and cold cuts — were rationed because of the war.
Each person was given a certain number of coupons for an item. The
allotments were very small and often the item was not available. But
sometimes you could get things that normally were rationed. In the
mornings, people lined up at bakeries to get fresh buns. I used to line
up and, if I was lucky, I would get a bag full of kaiser rolls, which we
all loved. My mom would fry onions with some red paprika; the fresh
buns filled with these finely cut fried onions were a real delicacy.

But now we were locked in the Jewish house with no chance of
escaping. The following week, that changed for me. One day before
noon, our house superintendent came to our apartment with a man
in civilian clothes in the style that Hungarian detectives wore. The
superintendent, in a high-pitched voice, said that this guy had a
document that ordered me to go with him to work with the International Red Cross. I have to point out that any Hungarian kid from
the age of twelve had to belong to a paramilitary organization called
the Levente. I had attended a number of this organization's meetings.
The meetings had two parts: disciplinary training and emergency
work, for which we were taken to clean building sites that had been
bombed. So when I saw this detective type, I connected him to my
Levente activity. My mother got really scared, not knowing what this
order meant. The man discreetly told my mother to give me a coat
or sweater where the yellow Star of David was fastened with pins

for easy removal. This gave my frightened mother a clue that he was friendly. So I said my goodbyes and went with him.

As soon as we left my house, his eyes searched the area to see if it was safe, and when he seemed satisfied, he told me to remove the yellow star. He told me he was a member of my Hanhac organization and that he was taking members of my *kvutza* from the locked Jewish houses to an office that was part of the Zionist underground. This was my first encounter with one of our group wearing a disguise. I learned later that wearing some sort of uniform as a disguise gave members freer movement on the streets of Budapest, especially during air raids.

He took me to an office building on Mérleg utca, a street in the prestigious business district close to the Danube. When we arrived, I met some of our leaders and also some members of my *kvutza*. It was both a happy and a sad reunion: happy because we were together again, sad because of the unknown future awaiting our loved ones. One of the older leaders welcomed me and told me that in the evening we would be taken to an address in Buda, where we were to stay until we received further instructions. He looked me over and asked if I had brought any clothing or other supplies. I told him I didn't have anything with me because I wasn't told to bring anything. He said that the man who had brought me from my house hadn't understood his instructions and that the office would prepare a document for the superintendent of the building stating that the work I was reporting for would take a number of days and would require that I bring some supplies with me.

When the superintendent read this document, he became irritated. He said he didn't like it and wouldn't let me leave the house. I started to cry and then I shouted that if I didn't appear at the place I had been ordered to go to, I would be in big trouble and so would he. After quite a lengthy shouting session, he finally let me go up to our apartment to get the stuff I needed. Of course, my family — my

father, mother, Suci and Jenö (who was now there on furlough) —
was elated to see me, especially when I told them what I had found
when I got to our Mérleg utca office. I said my goodbyes again and,
with tears in my eyes, left them there. My father, only fifty-two years
old, looked like a tired old man. That was the last time I saw my dear
father and my eldest brother, Jenö.

When I returned to the Mérleg office, I saw a very distinguished
gentleman. I was told it was Dr. Ottó Komoly, the head of the Hungarian Zionist Association, Hanhac and the Relief and Rescue Committee. We heard that he had daily meetings with high-ranking German
and Hungarian officers or officials. Before liberation, he disappeared
from one of these meetings. No one, to my knowledge, found out
exactly what happened to him.

I also met our organization's main leader, who was nicknamed
Dajnus. His full false name was László Dunka, but his real name was
Dr. Billitzer. He was an ordained rabbi. He and his sister, Bracha, the
secretary treasurer of the organization, managed all our activities,
and in Dajnus's attaché case was a pile of false documents for us to
use in our underground activities. I was told that Dajnus had been
arrested a short time after the occupation. He had been taken to SS
headquarters in Buda. They interrogated and tortured him for weeks
to get information about the underground. He never broke down.

A huge amount of money had been offered to the influential Hungarian detective chief to get Dajnus released, without success. Then,
in July, a Swedish diplomat named Raoul Wallenberg arrived. He
came up with a unique and very effective idea called the *Schutzpass*
or protective passport, which stated that the bearer of the document
was a citizen of Sweden and under that country's protection. Soon,
other neutral consulates in Budapest — Switzerland, Spain, Portugal
and the Vatican — began to issue such passes to Jews. Raoul Wallenberg tried to save as many Jews as possible from the claws of the
fascists, issuing thousands of *Schutzpässe*. One of the first protective

documents from the Vatican was for Rabbi Billitzer. It freed Dajnus from the clutches of the German interrogators. After a short rest and recuperation, he returned to lead his underground organization.

My arrival at Mérleg utca was not long after Dajnus had returned to active work. Since the Germans had shaved his head, Dajnus now pretended to be a priest. I couldn't believe the different disguises our members used. As I waited with a number of my small group in the Mérleg office for transfer to our new hiding place, a police sergeant in full uniform with the customary revolver and sword came in looking for Dajnus. I became somewhat panicky until a veteran of the place told me that the policeman was Dajnus's relative, and the two of them were going to a holding place where Jews were taken after they had been grabbed on the street for "crimes" like covering their yellow stars, reading a newspaper or similar serious felonies. When our group received information that some of our members or their families had fallen victim to such arrests, Dajnus and his cousin went to release them with some false but "good" documents.

That evening, we headed out to Buda and our new hiding place on Orsó utca. Orsó utca was unique as all the villas until then had been owned and occupied by Hungarian aristocrats or very wealthy families. In the aftermath of the German occupation, the SS authorities had seized the whole street from its original owners and established a secondary command post there. In the midst of all these famous villas, a new villa was built and the owner agreed that it could be used as a safe house for members of our organization. We succeeded in getting the International Red Cross and the Swiss consulate — two institutions the Nazis actually respected — to put protective signs up in front of this villa. German command cars sat day and night in front of our villa and drove up and down the entire street.

When we arrived, the villa was dark because the electricity was off. Yet, I could see that the many rooms of the building were packed. I knew only a few of those inside. The majority were members of the Hanhac from different towns in Hungary — from the Hungarian parts of Transylvania, the Subotica area of Yugoslavia, Pozsony and Košice in Czechoslovakia, and from other towns I was unfamiliar with. Every single one of them had a story to tell. One especially comes to mind, that of an older (relative to my age) individual in his mid-thirties who kept very much to himself. He walked with a limp. From time to time, he disappeared for days and then reappeared again. After the war ended, his mystery finally came to light in a magazine article. He had been a newspaper writer with leftist leanings and joined an underground group that supplied information to the Allied forces by radio. The authorities found out and captured him along with his radio. He was interrogated at length, probably without much success. Then he was given the death sentence. While being transported by train to a jail for the execution, he succeeded in jumping from the train and escaped. In the jump he broke his ankle, which left him with the limp. His subsequent disappearances were explained when I read that he was part of a small group put together to follow the deportation trains. These guys carried with them documents from different neutral consulates, documents that were, for the most part, still respected and obeyed. At pre-arranged stops they would contact the transport officer to whom they presented documents for some of the deportees, usually members of our organization, who would then be released to them. These fellows needed nerves of steel in their efforts to save individuals from certain death.

My Double Life and Tragedy

It was October 22, 1944, when our detective friend removed me from the Jewish house, and I was with my Hanhac Zionist group when a tragedy overtook my family. Usually males under or over the army age who lived in the designated Jewish houses all had to wear a large yellow star. Then, in October 1944, there was a coup by the fascist Arrow Cross Party and the rules changed: The Hungarian authorities came to the Jewish houses to pick up any Jewish male from sixteen to sixty years old for the forced labour units.[4] This included my middle brother, Jozsef (Suci), and my father. Jozsef was just past sixteen, and my father was fifty-two years old. My eldest brother's army document saved him from being taken away at that time. My mother's feelings on that occasion cannot be described: from eight of us, she was left with only my brother Jenö for a short while. Not knowing if she would ever see any of us again, it must have been extremely hard for my dear mother to endure her strong feelings.

A few days after the induction of my father and Suci, another group of policemen came to the house we lived in then. This time, they weren't regular police units. They belonged to the new regime in charge — the fascist Nyilas, or Arrow Cross, government. They didn't accept the military papers from Jenö's unit commander. They took Jenö, and we never heard from him again. The tragic irony of it is that

---

4 The age limit for the forced labour service changed throughout the years of the war.

almost all of Jenö's unit came back after World War II ended. Their decent commander had protected them as their unit followed the Hungarian army and went to the Ukraine. When the Soviets turned the war around, the German and Hungarian army units started to retreat, pursued by the Soviet army's trucks or horses. When the unit arrived at the Hungarian border area around August or September 1944, all the members of the unit were in rags. They had no decent footwear or clothing.

OMZSA — Országos Magyar Zsidó Segitö Akció, the National Hungarian Jewish Aid Association — was an organization that was able and ready to supply some of their needs. The unit's highest officer selected three soldiers and three members of the unit to go to Budapest to get the badly needed supplies. These six, which included Jenö, were all equipped with the necessary documents that should have protected them from the different authorities.

Jenö, just twenty-three years old when he perished, had only wanted to help his fellow comrades. He was the most decent human being and was a modern religious young man who had studied in a yeshiva, a religious school, in a distant town where the rabbi was an authority in higher learning. From the start of World War II, Jenö had always been involved in some type of assistance organization.

A week later, my father and younger brother, Jozsef, with the rest of the Jews who fell within the new ages for service in the forced labour battalions, were taken to a school building, which became the unit's camp. From there, the unit was marched daily to different locations in the badly bombed city of Budapest. The large group was directed and watched by a few soldiers. During one of the marches, when the unit had to turn a corner to the next street, my father pushed Jozsef out of the unit. They had planned this move in advance. First, my brother removed the yellow star and yellow armband and the military headgear, the only item supplied by the army. Then he went in search of my sister Edith. Edith had found out the location of our father and brother's unit and kept in contact with them.

From the early days of the occupation, Edith had pretended to be a Christian. Her fiancé's parents, the Grofs, had a devoted live-in maid who had been with the family a good number of years. One of the new regulations after the occupation forbade Jews to employ any Christian help. As the girl was from a small town in Transylvania and roughly the same age as Edith, it was arranged that she would return to her home, put together her documents and send them back to the Grofs. To move freely on the streets of Budapest, you needed a birth certificate and a police-registration slip. Anyone who came to Budapest for more than forty-eight hours had to register at the closest district police station and obtain a document that set out all the data about the registered individual with his or her exact address. If someone moved to a different location in the city or out of it, the same registration and document had to be carried all the time. Anyone of army age had to have the appropriate military papers. If you were employed, then you had to have a document of employment.

Edith coloured her dark brown hair blonde, made document-size pictures of herself and exchanged them with the ones on the maid's documents. She learned to speak and behave as if she came from the maid's district. My sister had finished high school and had beautiful handwriting, so she had to force herself to learn the right nuances so as not to give herself away. She found a job in a sizable printing company. When she went for the job interview, she was asked lots of questions, which she handled well. Then she was given a form to sign. My sister forgot her game; she signed the maid's name but neglected to write it the way the maid would have. The manager looked at the signature a few times, scaring my sister to the core, but he said nothing. In fact, he was very helpful to her when she needed to go somewhere during work hours. In short, he was a decent human being who didn't try to take advantage of the situation. Rather, he helped her when she needed help. So when my brother ran out of the marching line, he knew where to find Edith.

My sister, in the meantime, had learned from our Hanhac office about my brother's pending escape and received a set of papers suitable for him. After meeting my brother, Edith's first concern was to find a job for him so he could manage himself financially. My brother's papers indicated that he had come from a small town he'd had to flee before the arrival of the advancing Soviet army, and in the ensuing panic, had been separated from his family and so had come to Budapest.

My sister took a chance and brought my brother to the company she worked for and to the manager who'd hired her. She explained to the manager that she'd met him in a restaurant where he told her his sad story. She'd felt sorry for him and had brought him to the manager's office to see if he would have a job for him. The manager hired him without too many questions. My brother now had some income to support himself. Even more importantly, he would have the documentation this employment provided. Jozsef looked older than his sixteen years, and thus would be constantly stopped by the authorities to explain why he was not in the army. Fortunately, the printing company was designated as a defence department supplier, which gave a privileged status to their workers.

Being on the streets of Budapest could involve being searched, where the quality of the document could mean life or death. The searches had a special frightening name in German — *razzias* — meaning roundups. A police or army force would suddenly cordon off a street on both sides. Anyone falling into the area had to go through the two checkpoints and all their documents were scrutinized. The purpose of the search was to find Jews with false papers; army deserters or people who avoided the draft; members of outlawed organizations like communists or social democrats; and illegal refugees of neighbouring countries.

To ensure that no one escaped a *razzia*, the entrances and exits to the nearby houses and shops were carefully watched. That's why each of us from the underground had to have documents that were as authentic as possible. Usually our papers were based on one important and true document, such as a birth certificate or a police-registration document — these real papers were either provided by people who didn't share the regime's goals, or they were purchased from willing sellers. All of these people were taking great risks, as anyone caught helping the Jews would be severely punished, or worse. As for us, when we were questioned or searched, we had to control our fears and play the role our documents dictated. If someone seemed too nervous or sweaty, or the documents didn't seem right, the inspecting soldier or policeman would call an assistant who would take the suspicious individual into the entry corridor of the closest building. Here, the suspected individual was ordered to drop his pants to check whether he was circumcised, as only Jews were. If he was, it meant the end of his freedom and often his life. We lost quite a few of our comrades to such *razzias*. For our girls, it was a little bit easier. If they didn't show nervousness or fear, even if their documents didn't stand up to scrutiny, they usually were able to survive such searches.

I got permission from my leaders to take my brother to the Orsó utca villa as a temporary solution. A short while after Jozsef's arrival, a group of four heavily armed fascists came to the villa supposedly to take us to the Budapest ghetto, which had been recently established in the predominantly Jewish section of the town. The more mature girls of our group entertained these thugs. Lots of special foods and drinks were served to them until by the afternoon they were very drunk.

My brother was worried that they would find out that he had escaped from the forced labour unit, which carried the death penalty. So we left the villa and went to my sister's place. Now she faced a new problem: to find a place for Jozsef to live. In Budapest, it was a widely accepted custom for people to rent beds to people who came from out of town for a visit or for work. Usually such offers were posted on the entry door of the apartment buildings. After a few tries to find a relatively decent set-up, they ended up with one where other refugees rented beds.

I had a number of options for a night's stay. After I returned to the villa, I was asked if I was willing to come to the main office daily to do some courier jobs. I eagerly agreed. Under the sign of an international refugees' office, the organization rented a large apartment. This building, centrally located at the intersection of Rákóczi út and József körút, Joseph Ring Road, right beside the national theatre, once housed the main offices of the city's most important newspaper. Now, it served the fascist Arrow Cross Party newspaper. This place hummed with guys in uniform. There was hardly any uniform in Hungary that our guys didn't wear — soldiers of different ranks, policemen, streetcar conductors and others. Our city was still often attacked by air, and sirens would herd everyone to the bomb shelters. People with uniforms or other clear identification, like priests or doctors, could move around better by giving reasons for their activity to the house security wardens. Our chief, the rabbi, became a priest, as I mentioned. Some members who were in different stages of medical school became doctors. These positions were indicated by an armband. Of course, these "doctors" carried actual medical cases and many times were called to help out wounded citizens, especially after bombings. A priest had to provide the last rites for dying wounded. I had a paramilitary uniform with an armband of a cyclist courier unit. This uniform was made up of a special windbreaker, khaki shorts and shirt, and a special hat.

After my extraction from our Jewish house and the disappearance of my father and two brothers, my mother was totally alone. A short time later, some uniformed Hanhac men came with the appropriate document to take my mother with them. She didn't panic this time, as my experience had shown her that whoever came for her might be a friend and a saviour. She was taken to a suburb, to a camp on Columbus Street that had been established by Rudolf Kasztner, who was one of the major players in the Zionist leadership. He had been negotiating with the German high command to save as many Jewish lives as possible in the remaining days of the war. He negotiated successfully to save about 1,700 Jews, who were sent out of Hungary by train to safety. Also, Dr. Kasztner was instrumental in sending between fifteen and twenty thousand Jews to Austria, where most survived. Kasztner was one of the heads of Budapest's Jewish Aid and Rescue Committee (Va'ada Ezra v'Hazalah), which worked together with community leaders, but it was the committee who did the real work and effort of somehow helping and trying to save as many lives as possible. The Zionist leaders negotiated constantly with the Germans; I don't know what Kasztner promised to the Germans, but some of his negotiations worked, and he saved lives. However, after the war, Kasztner was accused of collaborating with the Germans. I believe that this was very misunderstood. I think that it was easy for people sitting in a courtroom in Jerusalem — the site of Kasztner's trial — to pass judgement, ashamed to some degree about what kind of resistance had not happened in Hungary. There was no military uprising in Budapest, as there was in the Warsaw ghetto. But they didn't understand that the needs and the circumstances dictated totally different activities than what happened in the Warsaw ghetto. In the Warsaw ghetto, the fighters knew that they had no chance, they knew what was waiting for them. But in Budapest the situation was totally different. Here, an uprising may have created a number of nice heroes, but they would have been dead heroes. Instead, we continued to work underground to save hundreds of thousands or more; that was our decision. Kasztner really was trying to save, not just Hungarian Jewry, but the last remaining segment of European Jewry. Yet, he was taken as somebody who had sold his soul. For someone like me, who lived through the period and was active and knew what was happening, this was a ridiculous thing.

~

After I found out that my mother had been taken out of the Jewish house to the Columbus camp, I would go and visit her there. Not far from the camp was a kiosk selling fruit and sweets. From the kiosk, I would buy things I knew my mother liked and didn't get in the camp. The trips to my mother's camp were fairly risky. Moving around Budapest was generally dangerous for Jews, but the trip to visit my mother added an additional element of risk. The streetcar that took me to the vicinity of the camp passed the eastern railway station, which was one street from my old house. I was afraid that someone from my neighbourhood would recognize me, which could end in disaster. A chance encounter with a neighbour was always a possibility anywhere in Budapest, but when I needed to cross my own area, the risk increased greatly.

On my earlier travels by streetcar to my Orthodox school, we kids developed a game that helped me in the double life I now led in the underground. A streetcar ticket was good for one week. It showed numbers for the year, month and week as well as for the hours the ticket was used. When the ticket was first presented, the conductor would punch in that week's number and the ticket was then only usable on the designated week. Our game was to avoid the conductor as much as possible so as not to have too many punched holes. This game served me well in my underground travels. It trained me to observe the passengers and the conductor entering or leaving the streetcar. As only gentiles were supposed to be in the city, we had to learn their habits. Hungary was and is a staunch Catholic country. Hungarians, when they passed in front of a church, crossed themselves and said the appropriate blessing. We, of course, followed this habit so as not to draw any attention to ourselves. We also later learned from our older members to be on the last platform of the streetcar as this sometimes provided a chance to get off from the side of the streetcar not in use and disappear before a *razzia* fully developed.

∼

After my brother Suci escaped his unit, my sister Edith attempted to rescue our father. Suci was able to provide information about the kind of set-up that existed at the site of his unit's camp, a school in Budapest. At my underground office, we prepared the necessary documents: first, a *Schutzpass* in my father's real name, in the hope that this would suffice to get him out; then, a set of gentile papers in case he had to be moved through the city. For my sister Edith, all these approaches carried a great amount of danger. She appeared as a Christian trying to help a Jew, which could have caused trouble for her if any of the guards turned nasty. Luckily, Edith was an expert at how to handle soldiers, who were usually village boys. One fateful Thursday, Edith made an arrangement with the guard on duty that she would be able to get my father out. The guard sent another soldier to bring my father to meet my sister. When my father arrived, Edith told him the plan. To her surprise, my father didn't want to hear about it. His explanation was that their officer had told them that all the men over fifty years of age from his unit would be released the following Monday. Apparently, the authorities found them to be more of a burden than a help.

In light of this development, he didn't want to endanger Edith and himself with the plan presented to him. My father, like most Hungarian Jews, was extremely law-abiding. He preferred to do things officially. So Edith prepared everything for the Monday release, but when she arrived at the school on Sunday, she found it deserted — the whole unit had moved out. After inquiring, it became apparent that the unit had been directed toward Germany. Edith became panicky. She asked around until she discovered that the unit had been put on a train to go to the Austrian border and ultimately to Germany. All this happened when Budapest was almost totally surrounded by the Soviets.

Edith tried to catch up with the train that carried our father, carrying the *Schutzpass* and other documents. During this trip, she was confronted many times by fascists asking what interest she had with a Jewish transport. Luckily, she was shrewd enough to find some excuse to allay their suspicions. But Edith never caught up with our father's train, and his exact fate did not become known to us until after the Soviet liberation. Edith blamed herself that she should have been more forceful with our father in the first place, but really the problem boiled down to my father's total obedience and Edith's respect for our father. My dear father was always as straight as an arrow, and that cost him his life.

The Underground Courier

My job as courier was to carry documents like *Schutzpässe* or necessary supplies to different hiding places in various buildings, such as a synagogue with proper protective symbols or schools or other public institutions not functioning because of the war. Some documents were for members of our group who were living in rented apartments. They needed good cover stories as to why guys of army age were not in the army. It was especially tricky for them during air attacks when everyone in the building had to get down to the bomb shelter.

I was on my way to one such place when I witnessed one of the most gruesome scenes of my courier activities. The street I was on was tree-lined on both sides with wide sidewalks. The Soviet army had captured the Buda side of the city and had sat there for close to two months, in what came to be known as the Siege of Budapest. They would shell the city with long-range cannons. As I progressed toward my designated address, I saw only one other individual walking in the opposite direction on the other side of the street. There was maybe a hundred metres between us when there was a huge bang. A Soviet cannon shell hit this other person, severing his head. His body took a step or two before collapsing. I was in shock; I could hardly move. When I arrived, the guys in the apartment thought I was a ghost. I couldn't even speak. Somehow, I came back to myself and was able to describe to them what I had just seen. Later, I saw many more such horrid occurrences.

The organization's leaders had quite an extensive list of connections in many important places. One of them was in the district police station. A number of times we were told by phone to be ready as a search party was on its way. Everyone from the office would disappear except for a gentile woman who was the office secretary and another gentile office helper. Most of us went to a nearby movie theatre that was showing news items from the different warring countries.

Our office never stopped working: It operated from morning until late at night. It was an excellent place to spend a few hours. It was heated and, if you could afford it, you could get some snacks. In the office, we saw two kinds of uniforms — the fascist Arrow Cross uniforms and German uniforms.

The head office of the Arrow Cross was at Andrássy út. The place became infamous for the terrible tortures inflicted on individuals who were brought there. It was said that it was easy to get in but almost impossible to get out. One of our older members was in his fourth year of medical school. On a trip to some meeting, he came face to face with a close friend from the university who was not Jewish and not a little surprised to see his Jewish friend. After some talk, our member understood that his old classmate was still his friend. Our member asked his friend what he was doing as a doctor now that he had graduated. He told our guy that he worked at Nyilas headquarters on Andrássy út, and that he did the medical checkups for new volunteers. Our guy, now trusting his friend, told him of our difficulty in getting Arrow Cross uniforms, documents and weapons, which would greatly help us save lots of lives. For that, his friend suggested a solution. He would take a day off from time to time, and our guy would substitute for him. Since he was near graduation as a physician, it wouldn't be difficult for him to take his friend's place. Then on those days he could arrange for some of our guys to pass the physical and become a part of a small unit of our own: a Nyilas group with a special purpose.

At that time, the Arrow Cross didn't accept the credentials of some protected houses. If that was the case, they marched the Jewish occupants of the house to the Danube River, forced them to undress, tied groups of them together with ropes and then shot them and threw them into the river. Tying them together ensured that if one was not fatally shot, he would be pulled down by the dead bodies and drowned.

When one of our sources notified us that such an event was about to take place, the new unit swung into action. They would go to the Danube with some bogus document to stop the massacre. This put enough confusion into the Arrow Cross ranks to cause some doubt and allow our unit to leave with the Jews. The Jews who had been saved were taken to various protected places and supplied with what they needed. Sometimes the Nyilas figured out that something was wrong and succeeded in wounding or killing some of our guys. In any event, those uniforms saved a lot of lives thanks to a true friend and human being.

In our Hanhac underground, the older members courageously performed extremely dangerous actions to save hundreds from certain death. Some of them went to detainment centres with falsified orders to pluck out arrested members or their families. Some went in uniform with special orders to release truckloads of people who were destined for deportation. They transported large numbers of Jews from one protected house to another when the first house became too dangerous. And they achieved all this in a lawless city without proper means of transportation.

They also fed a large number of people by carrying supplies in horse-drawn lorries through a city that was literally starving to death. Any wounded animal, whether a horse, a dog or a cow disappeared in five minutes flat, including the bones. Given these conditions, the lorries' contents had to be guarded with their drivers' lives.

The goal of the underground leaders was to save the last remnant of European Jewry. The Zionist organizations could acquire weapons and some had them, but the leadership always overrode the use of violence; they recognized that any confrontation, even if it killed the enemy, could result in an untold number of innocent Jews being killed in retaliation.

After the fascists took over the government in October 1944, there was no law in the city except that which was enforced by the weapons of the Nyilas forces. One morning when I left the villa, on my way to catch the streetcar to our office, I noticed two Nyilas soldiers some distance away. Our villa's exit door was down the main road from the streetcar line. As soon as I disappeared from the Nyilas' view, I ran down the slope in the hope of reaching the main road with the streetcar where there would be lots of people to provide me with a chance to escape. As I arrived at the bottom of the street, I noticed a large crowd surrounding something. I circled the crowd so I could watch the street. As I moved closer I saw two soldiers on the ground; they had been shot to death by a young Nyilas. One was a private and the other was a lieutenant colonel. In the Hungarian army, you had to be quite old to achieve such a high rank. When I asked what had happened, I was told that the Nyilas and the young private had had some argument after which the Nyilas shot the private. The lieutenant colonel arrived and questioned the Nyilas as to why he had killed the soldier. Without warning, the Nyilas then shot the officer. Of course, nobody had the guts to question the Nyilas' actions — that was the extent of this lawlessness. Meanwhile, the big crowd allowed me to disappear and catch the streetcar to the office.

We were ordered not to carry any weapons on us. One of my friends, somewhat older than me, didn't heed this warning. On one of my trips by streetcar to the office, we stopped at a busy streetcar exchange that took people into the Buda Mountains. Suddenly, from where I was standing on the last entry platform of my car, I saw my friend being led away by two Nyilas soldiers with bayonets extended, carrying the weapons they had found on him. I instinctively turned around so as to avoid being seen by my friend. God forbid, he definitely could have given me away. We never heard from him again.

Almost every day, I visited my mother in the Columbus camp. One day, the kiosk owner told me that I shouldn't approach the camp; in the morning, the fascist troops had marched out everyone in the camp in two columns. One column consisted of younger people, the other of older people. I was terrified as to what might happen to these two groups. Later, when some soldiers came to the kiosk, the owner asked them what had happened to the camp. The soldiers told him that the older ones would go to the ghetto and the younger ones would be marched toward Germany.

I was in a panic; in our underground grapevine, we were told that the ghetto was mined and would be blown up if the situation became critical. So I went to my sister Edith's. She had just been told that our mother was in the ghetto by one of the women whom my mother knew in the camp, someone with whom my mother had discussed her children's involvement in the Zionist underground. My mother had given her information on how to contact my sister, and this woman escaped as soon as the ghetto housing was arranged for my mother's group. My mother hoped that my sister would contact our organization and that it would be able to rescue her from the ghetto as well as provide my mother's friend with a hiding place and some false identity papers.

The three of us went to the József körút office. We told Bracha, our leader's sister, what had happened and how worried we were about my mother being in the ghetto. Bracha told us that to remove someone from the ghetto we needed someone dressed in a German uniform who could speak German. As we talked to Bracha, we noticed that Dajnus, our leader, was having a discussion with an SS officer. The doors between the two rooms were panelled with glass, allowing us to see the officer and Dajnus having a discussion. When we asked Bracha what was going on in the other room, she said the guy in the SS uniform was a real German; in fact, he was a German Jew who had not been circumcised because his parents were quite assimilated. Even with their efforts to assimilate, German Jews were still treated like all the other Jews and killed. When he realized this, he decided to join the SS with the goal that wherever his unit took him, he would try to contact Jewish resistance groups to help them in whatever way he could.

Bracha said that to extract anyone from the ghetto required a German soldier, especially SS, whom the Hungarian fascists feared and would obey. Bracha asked us if we spoke German. My sister spoke some. Bracha introduced us to the German soldier. Edith told him how fearful we were about the ghetto and our mother's predicament. She asked him if he was ready to help, and he said he was.

In November 1944, the ghetto had been created by erecting walls with gates at the extreme end of the ghetto area. The gates were guarded by Hungarian police or by the Arrow Cross. My mother's address, 6 Síp utca, was right beside one of the walls and gates of the ghetto, just down the street from the main offices of the Jewish National Congress.

A new set of identity papers was created for my mother and carried by my sister. A special document was also prepared to authorize the SS officer to take my mother for interrogation. My sister was to go with the SS officer as close as one block away, where she would wait for him and our mother. I would be one block farther away, from which point we would take my mother to my aunt Elza, who was living as a Christian with her husband, Zoltán (Zoli), on the Buda side of the Danube, right beside the Horthy Miklós Bridge, now known as the Petőfi Bridge.

When our SS saviour arrived with my mother, our relief was unbelievable. We couldn't thank him enough. He kissed my mother and sister and disappeared lest someone become suspicious of this odd gathering. My mother told us that the SS saviour, firm and menacing with his automatic machine gun, had engaged in a shouting match at the ghetto gate with the Nyilas guard. Once he was allowed to continue to my mother's building, the house's superintendent responded as soon as he heard the SS soldier screaming my mother's name. My mother almost had a heart attack when she saw that an SS officer was coming to take her away. The officer, seeing her fear, told my mother to take with her in her purse her most important things, as she wouldn't be returning to the ghetto. This gave my mother a sign that the officer was a friend who had come to rescue her.

We took the streetcar to the vicinity of my aunt's building and walked to the address. My aunt and her husband rented the apartment from an army colonel who was absent. Their problem in this seemingly comfortable arrangement was that almost daily they had to go to the bomb shelter, where the other tenants asked all kinds of questions about them that they sometimes found hard to answer. In any event, my mother stayed with her sister Elza and Zoli. Elza's husband was a university graduate, a very learned individual. He was also quite religious; it was hard for him to adhere to his observances in his present circumstances.

Some time later, I received a communication from my sister that told me my mother had been relocated to my father's synagogue building on István utca and Bethlen utca, which had become a protected building. The tenants in my aunt's building were becoming more and more curious and suspicious of my aunt and uncle, especially after my mother's appearance. As I mentioned, Soviet forces had encircled Budapest, and between the daily air raids and the Soviet shelling from Buda, most of the basic services had been destroyed. By mid-December, very little public transportation still functioned. The water and gas services had been shut down. It was very hard to reach faraway locations like my sister's apartment.

As a courier for the Hanhac organization I had a special pass that allowed me to enter into any protected building or institution. One of the major centres and hiding places was on Vadász utca, Hunter Street. This was one of the first glass buildings in Budapest. The building belonged to Arthur Weiss, a wholesale glass manufacturer, and it served as his head office, showcase and storage space. Mr. Weiss apparently had excellent connections with the Swiss consulate and rented the building to the consulate. The Swiss consulate, headed by Carl Lutz, allowed its consular emblems to be placed over the entrance, thereby declaring that the building was under Swiss territorial protection. Lutz allowed the offices of the Glass House to issue the *Schutzpässe* and other protective documents. Huge lineups gathered daily to get those miraculous papers. Slowly, the different Zionist factions settled in the building.

The main glass building had three or four floors. Attached to the main building was a U-shaped house, creating a four-sided courtyard. The building became filled to the point of being overcrowded. It was equipped with a central kitchen for the large in-house population. At its peak, the house guests numbered over 3,500. Each Zionist group had its own designated section. I had a good number of relatives and friends in the Glass House. My sister Magda, who belonged to the Mizrachi Zionist group, was there, and the husband of one of my mother's sisters became the cook. An uncle and some cousins were there as well. One evening, I decided to spend the night in the Vadász Glass House with my sister and other relatives. That would turn out to be the last time I would see my sister until after the war; I never did find out if she stayed there and if that was how she managed to survive.

The following morning, we were awakened by screams and shouted orders, indicating that some not-too-friendly visitors had broken in. Apparently, it was the private action of a group of Arrow Cross fascists who had come in to extract whatever they could in money, jewellery or any other valuables. A few of them climbed on top of the three-sided warehouse roofs with their machine guns. The rest spread out in the building to push everyone outside into the courtyard.

I was in an especially nasty predicament. I was wearing the paramilitary uniform of the Arrow Cross as my disguise. I had to get rid of my army hat, armband and documents. I pushed the documents into my winter boots. I hid the hat and the armband in a place where I hoped they wouldn't be found. In the inside corridors some sheets of glass still remained on display. Behind me, an older gentleman was moving more slowly than the Arrow Cross thug liked, so he gave him a strong shove. The old man fell forward and knocked me right into one of the glass plates. The glass plate broke into pieces. I was wearing scout shorts and was cut badly in three places, particularly my right knee and toe. The blood was streaming out. The Glass House had a nursing station and I was directed there. The nurse did not have sufficient gauze, so she used some paper to bandage my wounds until the bleeding stopped. Meanwhile, the crazy fascist intruders continued their rampage. The leaders of the building began negotiating with the fascists to determine how they could get rid of them. The people of the Glass House were asked to give over necklaces, chains, rings, watches and money. The negotiations went on for many hours. In the meantime, I started to feel better. I retrieved my hat and armband and was ready to sneak out of the building at the first chance I got. Of course, I looked a mess, all bandaged up as I was. When at last I got the chance to sneak out, I went to our office on József körút.

When I arrived, everyone in the office urged me to find a place where a doctor could treat my wounds properly. I knew about an old-age home and hospital in Buda where there was a doctor related to Edith's future in-laws. I was able to go to this doctor only on the third day after I was cut. Because of our very poor food supply, when I got to the doctor, the wounds were all infected. So the doctor cleaned the wounds, applied some cream and bandaged them properly. He also supplied me with additional bandages and cream for later. I was grateful for his help. Tragically, two days after my visit, a group of fascists broke in and systematically slaughtered all the patients, doctors and nurses. They killed everybody in the last functioning Jewish hospital in Budapest.

After the doctor's treatment, my whole body started to itch. My skin started to dry in different places and then curl up except in the centre of those spots where the skin was held together by raw flesh. Staff at the office suggested that I go to the synagogue where I grew up; it was now a protected building, as I mentioned, half of which was being used as a hospital for anyone in the vicinity who needed help. They transported me to the Bethlen Synagogue, where my mother had also been previously transferred. Our reunion was an occasion for great relief. We hugged each other and cried.

When the doctors examined me, they discovered that the cream the doctor at the other hospital had given me contained mercury. I had gotten a second-degree burn that had caused my skin to dry and gave me tremendous pain. They wrapped me in bedsheets soaked in glycerine to soften the dry skin and alleviate the agony. They also gave me some medication and bandaged my wounds properly. It took a few days for me to find relief. This turn of events effectively finished my underground activities.

When I recovered, I started to explore what was happening at the Bethlen Synagogue. Part of the complex that had been the kindergarten and elementary school had become a hospital. As the city was under air and ground attacks, lots of people got hit and hurt. Many of them were brought to the hospital with severe wounds and passed away there. The waterworks were totally destroyed by the bombing and the water pipes had very little pressure, but we could get some water at night when the industries and institutions that still existed were shut down and stopped using the water system. The water was used for the operations of the hospital as well as for the needs of the patients. Those who were not hospitalized congregated in the synagogue sanctuary and in the ladies' sanctuary on the second floor. Almost no food was available in the last weeks before the liberation. From time to time, a little soup was given with a few noodles or vegetables floating on top. In order for the synagogue to accommodate the many hundreds of refugees, the pews were removed and everyone slept on the floor with whatever the individual could muster as a makeshift bed.

One entered the building complex (not the synagogue) up a wide staircase to doors that brought visitors to the main floor. This was one floor above the sanctuary. As you came in from the main entrance and turned left, you passed the congregational offices. On the right, all along the corridor, were large windows and at the end of the corridor was the door to the ladies' sanctuary. The windows faced the backyard of the sport fields, which now contained piles of pews and other furniture from the synagogue. As more and more deaths occurred in the hospital, the basement rooms were used as temporary morgues. When they became full, the dead bodies were stacked in the empty spaces on the sports field. So, to get to the ladies' floor, you couldn't help but see all the dead and frozen bodies. Luckily, all of this was happening in the winter, so no sicknesses burst out. It was enough that a few times a day we had to pass this horrifying scene.

Most of the occupants of the synagogue were young men who had somehow eluded or escaped from the forced labour battalions. Around Christmas 1944, my brother Suci came to us. He had made arrangements with our dear friend Daty to spend Christmas with her. My brother was afraid that the other bed renters would ask him questions about the Christmas holiday celebrations. As Suci had never been involved with our Christian neighbours, he had very little knowledge of their customs. He had never played with the neighbourhood kids, so he was not as street smart as he ought to have been in those last days of the war. Therefore, he decided to go to Daty's, where he would feel safe. My mother begged him to stay, but Suci, seeing all the escapees, felt uncomfortable; if any military or fascist unit entered the place, it would have been a disaster for him.

As no other transportation worked, he made his way to Daty's on foot. He never made it. When he didn't show up, Daty went out to look for him. She heard that at one of the nearby major intersections, the Hungarian authorities had discovered a communist underground unit. Fighting erupted and many died or were wounded. A witness told Daty that a young man happened to cross the intersection just as the firefight broke out and was shot dead. The fellow described how he was dressed and mentioned also that he was carrying a little bag.

Everything in the description matched my brother, even the small bag, which had contained a rarity — sugar — that my brother had managed to get for Daty as her Christmas present. When Daty came to us a few days later and told us what had happened, my mother almost collapsed. I couldn't believe that my brother, whom we had seen just a few days before, was not with us anymore. This was one of many tragedies I would face. It was devastating to find out that one of my closest friends, my own brother, had just perished in such a chance way.

The Last Days of Desperation

The winter of 1944 was a very cold one. As people were killed by bombs and other ways, they often stayed on the sidewalk where they had fallen, frozen into the ground. There were no services available to remove these poor souls to morgues or other proper places of burial. Through the synagogue windows, I saw the piles of bodies grow and the grotesque forms of the different deaths they had suffered. It was a horrible sight for an adult, let alone for a twelve-year-old kid. I had already had to grow up rapidly to survive. Still, to see badly wounded individuals begging for help without having the ability to assist them was truly awful. I had to remind myself that I had played my small part in our organization and done many things that had helped others. I had even worked the copying machine in the office, duplicating *Schutzpässe* to be distributed to our fellow Jews who needed them. Many Jews survived because of these documents, and I was party to their creation. To our great sorrow, though, there were also many users who had plain bad luck and the documents weren't sufficient to save them.

~

The situation in the synagogue grew quite desperate. With almost no water or food, people became sick. The only light came from candles in the evenings. One night, the quiet of the place was broken by loud screams and orders. A group of SS had entered the compound. They ordered everyone, including the ones in the hospital, to go outside. An SS officer went to the entrance door to the ladies' floor. A Hungarian soldier, his head covered with a paper bag with holes for his eyes and mouth, stood beside him, holding a lantern.

All of those outside were directed to walk in single file toward the door where the SS officer and the Hungarian soldier stood. As we passed them, the Hungarian soldier pointed to the people that had to be separated. The ones he pointed to went to the right and the rest to the left. All the ones that went to the right were men of army age and deemed deserters. They were removed from the building and, to the best of my knowledge, never seen again. The story of this selection is an ugly one. In the hospital, there was a young Jewish girl who had a Hungarian boyfriend. This guy frequently visited his girlfriend and had seen large numbers of army-age men. He had snitched to the SS, who sent the selection squad.

In the morning, a group of Hungarian Arrow Cross arrived and took over from the SS. With the SS guarding the doors, an Arrow Cross officer ordered everyone to stand; that they were old or sick didn't matter. He explained that we were required to follow his orders and do some exercises. He began with toe-touches, then switched to squats and push-ups, starting the specific exercise slowly and then increasing the speed. Of course, most of us, the very young or very old, or those weakened by lack of food and water, couldn't keep up and fell down. He ran like a maniac between the rows and those who fell were kicked in the head with his heavy riding boots. It was such an awful scene that even the SS guard by the door left his guard post and went out to the corridor. This went on for an hour and a half. Then the Arrow Cross and the SS disappeared. We breathed a collective sigh of relief. Lots of people needed medical attention for the wounds that this fascist animal had inflicted on them.

A few days after this horrible night and morning, we heard a huge explosion. In a few minutes, the building was filled with clouds of dust that choked us. Our floor had gotten a direct hit from Soviet artillery. There was a gaping hole on one wall, but luckily no one was injured. It took a long time for the dust to settle so we could start breathing normally again.

The lack of water to drink was our biggest worry. A few blocks from the synagogue was a streetcar garage. In one of the yards of this large complex was a well that contained drinkable water. Two things prevented us from stampeding there: The first was the fact that patrols of SS and Hungarians still roamed the area. It would be a disaster for anyone caught on the deserted streets, especially Jews. The second obstacle was the presence of Soviet fighter planes nicknamed "Rata." They were so small that they could fly between rows of buildings and strike at any moving targets. As the house-to-house battles kept on, the Rata kept enemy troops off their soldiers and all civilians off the street. But the water problem became so acute that a few of us decided to try the long dash to the streetcar garage to get some of the life-saving water.

In Hungary, there was a popular sparkling spring water called Kristalyviz, sold in bottles of about one and a half litres. The tops were equipped with an ingenious closing plug made of ceramic and wire combined with a red-rubber sealer. When the bottle was opened, the plug hung on the side of the bottle. To close it, the wire structure allowed the placing of the plug into the bottle opening and the wire then sealed the bottle automatically. This is the bottle we carried with us when we made our dangerous dash. As soon as we heard the noise of the Rata plane, we would paste ourselves against a wall. This saved us even if the plane struck the street we were on.

My mother made me swear that when I got the water, I'd take just one little sip. If someone who was extremely thirsty swallowed too much, he or she could get violently sick and even die. In spite of my desire to quench my thirst, I knew that I'd have to trust my mother's experience. Therefore, I just had a few little swallows at the well and again on my way back.

From the large windows of our synagogue, we watched the house-to-house battle being fought. Our synagogue on István utca was located at an important intersection. On one side, the Hungarian agriculture and veterinary school took up a whole block. On the corner beside it was the MABI (the abbreviation of Magánalkalmazottak Biztosító Intézete), the national health insurance organization for self-employed people, to which our family belonged. Our synagogue and school complex was on the third corner. The fourth corner was taken up by a large apartment building with a movie theatre.

The two corners of the veterinary school and the MABI became important strategic corners where Germans and Hungarians created strong positions to try to stop the advancing Soviet forces. The battle raged over a day and a half until the vastly stronger and better-equipped Soviet forces overpowered the Hungarian and German defenders. We kids watched everything happening outside very discreetly so as not to draw fire. We supplied our friends and families with news about when the expected breakthrough might occur. Eventually, we saw a unit carefully approaching our complex to check for possible enemy pockets. We didn't know what to expect from these battle-weary soldiers, but we waited patiently for them to come to us.

Liberation for us was on January 20, 1945. An officer with his platoon of soldiers burst into our room, our home for the last month. The officer looked around and then approached one of the older people and quietly asked, in Yiddish, if we were Jewish. "Of course," came the loud response. The officer put his finger to his mouth, signalling us to be quiet. Then he explained to the older gentlemen in Yiddish that his unit was from Ukraine and very antisemitic, and we shouldn't declare to them that we were Jewish in case they would harm us. "They don't even know I'm Jewish," he added. What hearing this meant for us is hard to describe. We had dreamed of the glorious welcome we would receive from the victors when they found out who we were and what we had endured as Jews. It was as if the coldest shower had been poured on us.

As the street fight moved toward the national park area, we slowly moved out to see if we could find something to eat. At the same time, the Soviets looked for items worth taking. They would burst into a store or warehouse, breaking the door or shooting it to pieces, looking for whatever caught their fancy. The people of the neighbourhood followed the Soviet soldiers and took anything that could be used for heating. Doors and window frames, shelving and anything like that was taken by the hungry and cold masses.

Close by our synagogue was a pub-style restaurant, in which the Soviets found a cellar with huge barrels of wine and beer. The soldiers shot open the barrels, drank as much as they could and left the rest for the crowds. Hungry and thirsty for such a long time, many people just couldn't resist this windfall and drank large quantities, which in many cases killed them. I had our large bottle and remembering my mother's stern warning, I brought back with me a jug of wine. But we still had no food. Half a block from our synagogue was a candy and sweets manufacturing plant. A few of us went to see if we could find anything to eat there. When we arrived, almost everything had already been cleaned out. In one corner, we saw people fighting to get close to a barrel. For the first time, we saw a Hungarian with a red armband, which meant he was affiliated with the Communist Party. When he saw what shape we were in and found out we were Jews who had survived, he used a stick to hit the people around the barrel to allow us to clean out what was still left. This barrel had been full of sugared orange peels. I found a carton-box top and used it to carry some of the most wonderful sugar-coated orange peels. There was nothing on earth that tasted as good as this newly found treasure. Like everything that we came across in the next few days, we rationed this out so as to make it last as long as possible.

A few days after liberation, my mother decided that it was time to go and see what had happened to our apartment. We were only three streets away from it. When we arrived, we saw that many people still lived in the bomb shelters, as if expecting that things could change.

Why take chances? We found our close friend and neighbour, Aunt Manci. She was overwhelmed with joy when she saw us. She knew that we had been through hell. She invited us to her section in the cellar, where she was cooking bean soup. After the feast, she told us that another family had moved into our apartment. But Manci and our superintendent succeeded in clearing the tenants from our home. We returned to the synagogue to salvage what we had and carried our belongings back to our apartment. We also explored the area near our building, but nothing was functioning yet. The American Jewish Joint Distribution Committee (the Joint) had established offices in the synagogue building, along with some storage rooms and a kitchen. This was positive news that would make our new lives somewhat easier.

In the early days of liberation, it was dangerous to move around the city. The half-destroyed city houses collapsed, blocking streets and passages. You had to make huge detours to get to any destination. Marauding Soviet soldiers were given a free hand by their officers after long months of heavy fighting. They would stop pedestrians and, in Russian, demand that they hand over their watches or be killed. A more serious danger faced young women. Many soldiers, drunk from the liquor found in stores and warehouses, abducted them and raped them. Younger females soon disguised themselves as older women to avoid being raped. This situation went on only for a few days after the liberation. Soon, Soviet military patrols took these excesses very seriously. There were on-the-spot executions for rape or serious robberies.

A few of us kids would roam the streets together, trying to find something to eat. Sometimes, when we came across a destroyed bakery, we climbed to the top of the ovens and found mouldy bread pieces. We scraped them relatively clean and ate from them what we could.

Soon after liberation, my sister Edith found us in our old apartment. She was living with her future in-laws, Dr. Grof and his family. They had a large apartment at 17 József körút, near our main underground office at 3 József körút. She told us that the Grof family was being forced to accommodate a Soviet general with his colonel wife, both doctors. They also had an escort and cook with them. This reduced their personal living space to a minimum. On the other hand, it brought security and some food supplies that other Hungarian survivors could only dream about.

The next day, I set out to visit Edith and the Grofs. My journey took me to the well-known Rákóczi út, one of the main streets of Budapest. It was a very wide street, so even the rubble of the destroyed houses didn't stop traffic on the road. Beautiful department stores and stores selling coffee and cake could be found all along the street. The morning of my visit, I passed a famous cake-and-coffee house called the Hauer and saw a big crowd around the freight entrance. On the street was a Soviet truck. A Soviet soldier appeared at the freight exit, carrying a burlap bag. As soon as he moved into the crowd, someone plunged a knife into the bag, which burst open, revealing a treasure of almonds that fell on the snow-covered sidewalk. Like a pack of hungry hyenas, the crowd jumped on this treasure and filled their pockets, bags, hats, whatever they could. The Soviet soldier just laughed and went back for another load. I succeeded in filling my hat and two pockets and left very happy. An elegantly dressed gentleman stopped me when he saw that I was eating almonds. He showed me a gold pocket watch and said that he would give it to me if I would give him a handful of my almonds. I gave him a small handful but declined the watch.

On my arrival, the Grofs invited me to have some food with them: cold cuts, which I hadn't seen in so long, good bread and even some milk. In short, a feast fit for a king. When Edith visited us, she saw that our mother had a bad infection on her knee. She needed the antibiotic streptomycin. The Grofs had already asked the general doctor, but he couldn't get it because the Soviet army needed it for their soldiers to treat the syphilis they had acquired through rape or other contacts they had had on the battlefields. The doctor suggested that my mother eat nourishing foods like bacon, sausages and butter, but that was just impossible. Even if such food had been available, my Orthodox mother wouldn't have eaten it if her life depended on it. The doctor said that if her infection didn't improve, she might require an amputation.

While we were talking about my mother's predicament, the general had a visitor. He was also a doctor, a colonel, and after a while it became apparent that he was Jewish. After hearing the story about my mother's problem, he summoned his driver, gave him some instructions and sent him away. Not long after, he invited Edith and me to his car and asked us to direct his driver to our house. When we went up to our apartment, the driver carried a good-sized box. As it was late Friday afternoon, the Shabbat candles were lit. When our colonel doctor saw this, he had tears in his eyes. He kissed my mother and explained in Yiddish that he had found some penicillin for her infection and had brought lots of nourishing foods: eggs, bread, flour and many other goodies in the form of jams and sweet things. My mother hurriedly prepared the Shabbat table where our guest and saviour had the most wonderful Shabbat dinner. We sang some Shabbat songs at our guest's request. It was one of the most memorable Friday nights we had had in a long time. The food this Soviet officer brought us lasted for a good stretch. It was like manna from heaven.

~

Slowly, some services started to operate. Trains took eager passengers to different destinations. One day, when I was with a group of friends out looking for food, we heard that some train cars way past the eastern station had salt in them. Lack of salt was an issue in many parts of the country. Even in the small towns or villages that produced their own food, salt shortage was a big problem. So a few of us went in search of these railway cars. We took some bags with us in case the rumour was true. To our great joy, it was. Three train cars held this precious cargo. We filled up our bags before we realized just how heavy the salt was. We poured some back little by little, until we felt that we could carry the bags to our homes, which were a fair distance away. It was tough going, but we knew it would be worthwhile.

We went to the railway station to find out in which directions the trains were moving; this would tell us in which villages it would be good to try to sell or exchange our salt. Then we divided the salt into half-kilo packages, a good amount for household needs. A few days later, three of us set out on our new business venture. The train ride progressed slowly, as many of the tracks had been bombed and railway crews were out repairing them to restore some semblance of movement for passengers as well as for supplies. The few trains that moved were always packed, even on the roofs. Many people slept in or around the station in the hope of catching a ride home.

Over a distance that in normal times took about two to three hours, we spent two and half days. We found a treasure of items to be gotten with our salt: buns, hard-boiled eggs, some cakes and sausages. As the train often stayed at a stop for a long time, the villagers ran home and brought back flour, butter, cheeses, green, red and yellow peppers and fruits like apples, pears and plums. Our backpacks slowly filled up with goodies before we got to our original destination. We didn't even need to trade away all the salt we had brought with us. So we left our train and waited to catch a train going back to Budapest. Although I was not yet thirteen, I had to learn ways and tricks of the market to sustain my mother and myself in the starving city of Budapest. There were plenty of rumours about residents of the city who became quite wealthy from expensive items they succeeded in stealing and hoarding.

After the storm of Soviet liberation had passed, I tried to find some connection to my Zionist organization, with minimal luck. Here and there, I met some members but nobody knew about any reorganization. Early in March 1945, we found out that some of my father's friends from his forced labour unit had come back to Budapest. We traced one of them, and from him we received the devastating news about my father. He had been killed on January 20, 1945, the exact date my mother and I were liberated by the Soviets. He told us what happened: My father's unit was brought to the Austrian border from the school in Budapest. The place was called Sopronbánfalva. The unit helped reinforce the border defence lines. Every morning, the unit was marched to the defence lines and put to work under the Hungarian soldiers who were assigned to them. My father was a small, fairly frail individual. Being a religious leader, he was assigned to the kitchen as an overseer of kosher cooking. It was now the bitter winter with lots of snow, especially on the mountain ridges where they worked. The army *keret*, cadre personnel, was made up of soldiers from the regular Hungarian army ranks. In my father's case, they were relatively decent. They demanded that the work assigned to the Jewish labourers be done properly but treated them as well as conditions allowed.

One day, a *keret* appeared from the Hungarian fascist organization, the Arrow Cross. They sent away the regular Hungarian soldiers and took over the unit. New orders were issued, with much harsher conditions. They forced everyone except the cook and his helper out of the kitchen to go to work. This included my father. As they marched up to the mountain to reach their workplaces, a strong snowstorm slowed them down considerably. These new Arrow Cross soldiers tried to push the unit faster so as not to waste time. Suddenly, my father fell into a hole covered with snow. The guard who was closest to him, without much hesitation, shot him. My father was not fatally wounded and some of his friends tried to reach and help him, but the guard warned them that anyone who attempted to help my father would be shot with him. Then he shot my father again.

Hearing this, it felt as if lightning had hit us. First, we had gotten news about my brother Jozsef's untimely death; then there was the disappearance of my eldest brother, Jenö; and now this news of my father's demise was almost unbearable. For days, my mother could hardly utter a word. My two sisters and I were the only ones she had left from our immediate family. It was the saddest period of my young life.

We slowly got information about the rest of our extended family. Except for one sister, who had died, my mother's other six brothers and sisters had survived and returned to Hungary. Their spouses and their children did not. Of course, we had no illusions about the survival of my mother's parents, my grandparents, whom we last saw at my aunt's wedding in the city of Vác. My grandfather was eighty-seven and my grandmother was eighty-two when the Nazis dragged them away as enemies of the state.

The first of my mother's brothers who survived and returned was my Uncle Jozsef, also from Vác. It was both a happy and sad reunion. He told us his story. He had been in a place called Bor in the Yugoslavian part of Hungary, which became a burial place for most of his forced labour unit, along with many others. Tens of thousands died there. My uncle, being a very religious man, would not eat non-kosher food. It was extremely hard to survive those conditions, but my uncle was able to live on roots, potato skins and similar vegetation.

When liberated, he started his return journey mostly by foot. His way back took him across Transylvania to a town that in Hungarian was called Nagyvárad and in Romanian, Oradea. He settled there for a few days of rest. With the return of survivors, he found that the place had a functioning synagogue. He met two similarly aged Jewish fellows and they became friendly. They lived in a sizable house belonging to one of them. As both had lost their young families, their lives felt empty. Even my uncle's arrival had lifted their spirits.

After resting for a few days, my uncle told them that he planned to continue toward his town of Vác near Budapest to see who had survived. When he mentioned his plan to then go on to Budapest, he was told that the city was literally starving. Yet, Nagyvárad was a city of plenty. It had anything you wanted in food and other products. Both men had already re-established their businesses. One had a wholesale business for sugar, salt, pepper, paprika, coffee and similar items. The second had a small jewellery store in one of the busiest parts of the city. They suggested that my uncle take with him as much foodstuff as he could carry, and they helped fill his backpack and a small suitcase. His two friends told my uncle that if he found a surviving family member who needed a place to recuperate, to put his or her life back together, he should feel free to count on them.

So my uncle left and returned to Vác to see if anyone was alive. Sadly, all he found were the empty houses of his family and parents, my grandparents. Then he continued directly to our apartment in Budapest. We hugged each other and cried from sorrow and from happiness for the good fortune of finding each other. The contents of my uncle's backpack and suitcase greatly added to the happy side of the reunion. But the stories of both sides were equally horrifying — what we each had gone through in order to survive!

My uncle quickly found a synagogue to his liking. My aunt Elza and her husband, Zoli, resurfaced and decided to settle in Vác. My aunt Ilonka and her daughter, Edith, arrived back from the concentration camps. Mother and daughter had supported each other, which had given them the strength to survive. Ilonka's husband, Edith's father, never returned. Another uncle named Zoli survived but lost his wife and two children. Most of our relatives stayed in Budapest or its vicinity. As religious Jews, they started to look for new partners, for husbands or wives.

With time, I succeeded in reconnecting with my Zionist organization, which had revived itself with the old goal of training youth to settle in Palestine. They started to have the customary Saturday meetings and the mid-week smaller group get-togethers. But very soon, the Zionist groups discovered that the new communist regime did not look favourably on such organizations. The only Zionist faction that was in some way supported was Hashomer Hatzair, a heavily left-leaning socialist group. They admired the Soviet regime as well as the Hungarian communist government. The rest of the Zionist factions went into a semi-underground mode.

Around mid-April 1945, while the goodies that my uncle had brought us slowly disappeared, my uncle convinced my mother that both of us should go with him to Nagyvárad, to his two friends, to recuperate from the war's difficult times. He said that my mother could manage the house for all of us. My uncle's two friends, besides looking after our needs, would probably pay my mother something, which would come in handy for when we returned to Budapest.

So we left Budapest and came to the nice spacious house with lots of room for all of us. The two men already had a steady cleaning lady who would now work with my mother. The men loved my mother's cooking and the way she brought order into their house. My mother tried to rebuild my physical health and to repair the damages starvation had caused, so she fed me like a locomotive. Each morning, I had a big bowl of cottage cheese with two or three eggs mixed in with lemon juice and lots of sugar, and in a short time, I showed improvement. The back of my neck had become infected from lack of vitamins and that began to heal.

My birthday, May 19, rapidly approached, and with it came the time for my bar mitzvah. I knew that I wouldn't have a real bar mitzvah because there was not sufficient time to learn the necessary parts. Also, there was no one to teach me my portion, so I had to settle for a Torah honour and say the customary blessing for such an honour. The contrast to my brother Jozsef's bar mitzvah three years prior was astounding. My father had taught all the upcoming bar-mitzvah boys, including my brother, back in those days. It had been a lavish celebration. My brother Suci's godfather owned a sizable bakery and during the three days of celebration, he constantly supplied us with cakes, cookies and challah for sandwiches. It was customary to bring presents for the bar-mitzvah boy. Pelikan pens were very popular and my brother got over thirty. But in May 1945, when my time came, the world had changed. Given all our tragic family losses, it was not the time for an elaborate celebration anyway, but as a youngster, I still felt the loss of this very important Jewish milestone.

Longing for our Dreams

After living in Nagyvárad for a while, one of the men, the jeweller, asked me if I would like to help out in his store. Of course, I happily agreed. I went daily with our friend and host to his jewellery store. As most of the buyers were Romanian officers, I became fairly good at talking to our Romanian customers, telling them our prices in Romanian. These officers loved fancy uniforms, colognes and jewellery, especially rings and chains of gold or silver. The store was usually busy and business was great. Some time after my bar mitzvah, the store owner noticed that we were running out of silver chains. The only place he knew where the stock of chains could be replenished was in Budapest. He asked my mother if she would allow me to go to Budapest and buy the chains from our supplier.

My mother was at first reluctant to let me go, as I had just turned thirteen and the trip — approximately three hundred kilometres — had to be done by hitchhiking on Soviet army trucks. But remembering the previous year and my life in the underground, she felt confident that I was up to the challenge. I looked forward to the chance to find out the status of my Zionist group and renew my connections to it. I was to carry a substantial amount of Hungarian currency for the purchase of the chains. This money was sewn into my coat, which was designed so that it would also serve as the hiding place for the purchased chains. When the day of departure came, some tears were shed and off I went.

I familiarized myself with the different towns I needed to pass through on my way to Budapest. The Soviet army mainly used old American Studebakers for troop transport, equipped with benches on either side. People congregated at designated exit points, patiently waiting for a truck going in the desired direction that had empty seats and a realistic asking price. I hopped on a truck that took us to a town not too far from Budapest. I jumped off that truck and joined a group waiting to get another truck into Budapest. After quite a while, a Soviet truck that was going to Budapest pulled up. The price was agreed upon and paid to the officer who sat beside the driver. The driver was erratic, going from side to side, often brushing the roadside trees. We told the officer that we were worried about our safety, but he just laughed. The truck would frequently stop for food, services and mainly additional alcohol. Finally, we noticed that we were in the suburbs of Budapest. By this time, the city streetcar and bus systems had been partially restored, so it was possible to get to our different destinations by public transportation. We all felt relief when we climbed down from the truck.

When I returned to our apartment alone, Uncle Jozsef couldn't believe his eyes. After some rest, I asked my uncle to accompany me to the chain supplier. I told him everything that had happened since he left us with his two friends. He blessed me for my bar mitzvah and voiced his sorrow that he could not attend. The next day, we went to my main supplier. Everything went smoothly, just as our jeweller friend had described it would. The purchased chains were hidden nicely in my coat without too noticeable a trace.

We also went to visit my sister Edith. She was in good shape herself, but the Grof house was an extremely sad place, despite the fact that the Soviet general and his entourage had left long ago. After I gave her a full report about how we were doing in Nagyvárad, Edith told us the reason for the heavy sadness. Toward the end of the war, the Grofs were hidden by good gentile friends and thus had survived the storm. Their only son, Laci, Edith's groom-to-be, was living with his cousin. The two of them had false papers and went to medical school to continue the family tradition of becoming doctors. Like many other Jewish university boys, they belonged to the socialist party. After this party was declared illegal, the list of party members was searched for. Despite their false papers, they didn't feel safe, so when they learned that the Soviets had reached the suburbs of Budapest, they decided to go to the Soviet lines and ask for asylum. The cousin, being from the Yugoslavian part of Hungary, spoke Russian and this — in addition to their being socialists — made them feel confident approaching the Soviets. So, after they said their goodbyes to the Grofs and my sister, they left.

For a long time, there was no communication from them. After the war ended, the Grofs became terrified as to what could have happened to their only son, since they knew that lots of people had died in the last days of the fight for the city. They turned to desperate measures. Ella Néni (Mrs. Grof) and Edith started to search the route they knew the two boys would have taken to reach the Soviet lines. After many gruesome days turning over dead bodies with no result, Mrs. Grof was too exhausted to continue this terrible search, and they resigned themselves to waiting until some news surfaced.

A few weeks later, the Yugoslavian cousin finally showed up and told a terrifying story. Instead of finding safety, as soon as they reached the Soviet lines, they had been arrested. No explanation or verification helped, and they were sent to a prisoner-of-war camp. During one of the transfers from one local camp to another, the cousin escaped. Meanwhile, Laci, the Grofs' son, had become sick with typhus. If he didn't get the right medication, he would die. The Grofs approached the Soviet general and his wife for help to get the medication to their son but they declined, having no authority in prisoner-of-war camps, so Edith herself went to the city where the camp was. She offered the guards money to take the life-saving medicine to Laci.

They refused, and she was warned twice that she would be shot if she didn't move away from the fence. Poor Laci passed away in that hell-hole of the Soviet liberators.

When they received this tragic news, the Grofs totally broke down. They even contemplated suicide; as a doctor, Mr. Grof had the means in his hands. If not for Edith, they would have done it, but she brought them back to reality. After some time, they insisted on adopting Edith as their daughter in place of their lost son.

It was a heartbreaking story. We all had similar tragedies to re-count, including the three avoidable deaths in our own family: my father, so straight of character; my younger brother, lost because of his fear of questions by strangers at Christmas; and my eldest brother, destroyed by his wish to help his comrades, most of whom came back while he perished. I was one of the lucky ones who survived.

~

After visiting the Grofs and my sister, I went to the Jewish centre of the city, hoping to find some connection to my organization. Eventually, I came across an older member who told me where and when meetings took place. At one such meeting, I was able to renew old connections and create new ones. The discussion's main thrust was planning the first post-war summer camp at Lake Balaton. I also finally met my first cousin Yehuda Benyovits, who had helped me join the Hanhac in 1940 and who had become a very important lead-er of the group. I told Yehuda about my family's losses, and how a few of us had survived the calamity. In turn, he told his sad story of the loss of both his parents and of his eldest brother, Miklos, dying in a forced labour camp. The rest of his family was already in Israel. I told Yehuda that my mother and I were staying in Nagyvárad temporarily, but that I intended to come back soon to be able to rejoin the Hanhac. Yehuda said that if I returned in time, he would include me in the group going to set up the campsite a week before the regular arrivals. In view of this urgency, I cut my stay by two days so I could work on my mother and on our two hosts.

The return was a lot smoother than the trip to Budapest had been. On my arrival, I was received as a hero. Considering that I had just passed my thirteenth birthday, I felt like a daring adventurer. My mentor, the jeweller, couldn't believe that I had accomplished the whole trip in such short time and with such success. He rewarded me handsomely and thanked my mother for allowing me to undertake such a complicated trip.

Shortly after my return, I told my mother about the Hanhac meeting and the fact that Yehuda had offered to send me to the youth camp with the preparatory group if I returned in time. My mother wasn't too thrilled by the idea at first, as she liked our set-up in Nagyvárad, but then sentimentality came into the decision-making. She was looking forward to seeing Edith and her brothers and sisters, and ultimately agreed that we could arrive in time for the camp job.

This provided me with three weeks of fun instead of only two as well as the prestige for having been chosen for such an important task. The camp belonged to the Catholic teachers' organization in Budapest. Part of it was in buildings, part of it in tents. The preparatory group had a number of jobs. First, the kitchen had to be put in good order. Then the buildings had to be cleaned and the tents' floors raked. We also had to build a stage for shows and games. But the major task of our group was to prepare the so-called mattresses: burlap bags packed tightly with straw. This was a lousy job. As we pushed the straw in, we scratched our hands terribly.

The camp was in the town of Balatonboglár. The Balaton is the "sea" of Hungary, some seventy kilometres long and about fourteen kilometres wide at the widest point. During the war years, lots of planes, complete with their pilots, were shot down into the Balaton — so, unbeknownst to us, the beautiful lake that we so eagerly looked forward to swimming in was polluted by rotting bodies. The main benefit to being at the camp a week earlier than the others was the pleasure the Balaton provided us, but by the second day, the whole preparatory group was covered with infected scratches. We got some cream to eliminate the itching and to counteract infection, but we couldn't enter the Balaton for the rest of the camp. It was a heavy punishment instead of a special status.

The camp was a wonderful experience, otherwise. It comprised two large competing groups, one from Budapest and one from Debrecen, the second largest town in Hungary. Each group had about five hundred kids and leaders. Judges gave positive or negative points to each group for singing, acting and cooking; all kinds of competition filled the time, along with recreation in the lake for those who had no scratches or wounds.

We also participated in serious discussions about issues, especially about what was happening in Israel (which, until its independence under David Ben-Gurion in 1948, was, as I mentioned, called Palestine by the British). All the different factions of Zionism had a single goal: to train the surviving Jewish youth for life in Israel, whether on kibbutzim or other forms of pioneering endeavours. Any news from the Land of Israel felt magical. After the Holocaust, the Zionist dream became the ultimate goal for many survivors. All the songs we learned and sang described life in Israel and our longing for our dreams to be fulfilled by making aliyah. Most evenings we spent around the campfire, dancing and singing our hearts out. This camaraderie and our common goals brought us very close.

After the camp's closing ceremonies, we felt elated and wanted to continue our training for the long-dreamed-of aliyah. In the meantime, Hungary became a full-fledged communist country in which Zionism was despised, so we were not officially recognized. Again, we had to find different ways to continue the Zionist enterprise. We had our mid-week meetings in whichever members' homes could accommodate ten to twelve kids — sometimes more — for lectures, discussions, singing and dancing. On Saturdays, we had the central meeting for all the *kvutzot*, which required an even bigger space.

At the end of December 1945 and the beginning of January 1946, rumours flew around about a group of youngsters setting out for Germany on their way to *Eretz Yisrael*. Yehuda approached us, suggesting that he take me in his group if my mother would consent to it. The group was to consist of about 120 orphans and half-orphans. Yehuda and his wife would accompany the group as well as a substantial number of other adults. It wasn't an easy choice, leaving my mother — who, a short time ago, had had a full house, humming with joy and laughter — totally alone. But in the end, she was ready to endure the loneliness in the hope that I would have the life I dreamed about. As solace, she knew that her brothers and sisters and Edith would be there if she needed help or company. So she gave her consent and blessing for me to join Yehuda and his group for the trip, first to Germany and, hopefully, from there to Israel.

The end of January was the date set for departure. I visited all those close to me to say goodbye. Edith was very sad but, like my mother, she understood that for me this was the culmination of six years' dreaming. All the other relatives blessed me and wished the whole group a successful and safe trip. My friends from the organization were both happy for me and the rest of the group and envious that they were not included on the trip.

When the day came, we got specific instructions where to meet and how to behave, as this trip was not too legal. We had Soviet soldiers to accompany us and they were supposed to deal with the authorities. This surprised us, but we later learned that our Soviet guards belonged to an underground organization called Aliyah Bet. This organization constantly searched for routes through Yugoslavia, Romania, Austria, Italy, France and many other countries to help Zionist youth escape Europe to Palestine. Many of the members of Aliyah Bet were discharged soldiers from the Jewish Brigade. We were transported by trucks to the railway station and put on a train to take us to the Austrian border crossing on our way to Germany.

In the aftermath of World War II, the world was full of refugees. They usually applied to the countries that were ready to accept refugees as displaced persons (DPs) in camps until their visa applications arrived. Refugees were supported by the UNRRA, the United Nations

Relief and Rehabilitation Administration. The only refugees who had to do everything clandestinely were the Jews who hoped to go to British Mandate Palestine. But continuing persecution against the Jews in Eastern Europe made us understand that the only solution for us was to return to our ancient land and rebuild it.

The Zionist goal was to gather together all the Jews willing to undertake the harsh life the homeland could offer at that time, to work the fields and reclaim them, and by building towns and villages, establish a renewed and viable Jewish country. In the territory called Palestine, there had always lived a substantial Jewish community beside its Arab neighbours. In my opinion, the only group on the mandated territory that could go back in history, name and language was the Jews. Our country's ancient name was *Eretz Yisrael*, the Land of Israel, as I have mentioned. Our language was Hebrew, revived after two thousand years to become a living beautiful language, usable in all facets of a nation's needs.

During and after World War II, there was much greater urgency to bring the survivors of the Holocaust to Palestine, so that they would feel at home and live in relative security. The British had maintained limited immigration until the mandate over Palestine ended in 1948. During all those tragic and fateful years, the British intelligence services and a considerable part of their navy continued to thwart these desperate masses from escaping the murderous Nazi regime.

∼

Our transport of 120 kids plus adult supervisors set out to reach our dream of Israel. Our first stop was Vienna. To get there, the train carrying us had to pass through Czechoslovakia. Our Soviet guards worked their magic and we passed the border with some delay but, in the end, successfully. We had now escaped the harsh communist laws and regulations in Hungary. In Vienna, we spent about two weeks in a building complex that, before the war, was the Rothschild Jewish Hospital. This complex now served as a transfer camp for Jewish refugees, mostly groups going toward Palestine.

Although some of Vienna was heavily damaged by the war, it was in way better condition than Budapest. We had a good time being shown many interesting places in this beautiful city. One memorable outing was to Schönbrunn, the seat of the Habsburg dynasty. It is one of the nicest European palaces, famous for its fantastic gardens.

All too soon, we were notified that army trucks would be driving us to another stopover camp. We were driven about three hundred kilometres to a displaced persons camp called Ainring near the Austrian-German border. Close to the camp fence ran an electric train that travelled from Austria to Germany. The camp was not the most cheerful of places. The barracks and other buildings were an ugly grey colour and some of the roads were just gravel.

Here, one could find Jewish survivors from various European countries waiting for visas to their dream destinations. Yet, some of the camp population sat there for a year or more after the end of the war. They tried to add to the meagre financial support from the UNRRA by buying and selling a variety of things. In Ainring, there was a relatively small group of Zionists waiting for permits. They spent their time learning Hebrew and arranging activities so as not to let their members do nothing.

About ten days after our arrival in Ainring, we were told to be ready the next morning to move on to our main destination. The customary army trucks came and took us to Aschau. During all our travels, we were supplied with food and drinks from the UNRRA. We never really needed to worry about or suffer from a lack of supplies. It was not fancy or luxurious food, but it was definitely satisfactory, especially compared to what was available in Budapest. But it became apparent that the Aschau camp we were being driven to was the wrong one. There are two Aschaus in Bavaria — Aschau im Chiemgau and Aschau am Inn, and the proper one for us was Aschau am Inn, near Kraiburg. When military communications revealed this to the convoy officer, the trucks started to roll again. We arrived at our destination quite late, so we couldn't see too much, but we were still able to notice the great difference between Ainring and Aschau.

The camp location alone was marvellous. It was situated in a valley between two lines of hills full of fruit orchards.

In the morning, we found ourselves in an attractive camp, relatively small in size, accommodating up to five hundred refugees. This contrasted with other DP camps with populations of five thousand to ten thousand or more. In addition, we were told that this camp was available only for organized Zionist groups. The camp was made up of small semi-detached units, each side having a large room for eight to ten people and a common toilet, shower and washing areas. There were also buildings for the kitchen, dining room, laundry room, storerooms and so forth. The dining room was large enough to have one sitting for the whole camp; it could also serve as a theatre with a stage or as a basketball court. Behind the dining room was a super-modern kitchen with stainless-steel pots and pans, tables and work surfaces.

After I familiarized myself with the camp, I had a pleasant surprise — I found my sister Magda and her newborn daughter! Meeting Magda there was fantastic. I'd had no knowledge of my sister's whereabouts, having lost almost all contact with her after the liberation in January 1945. We had a lot to tell each other and talk about, most of which was tragic, as we commiserated over the loss of our father and two brothers.

Unfortunately, Magda had married a fellow socialist underground member, Engel, who had given her a lot of grief almost from the beginning of their relationship. Magda had become pregnant shortly after their wedding and now she was pregnant again and he had left her.

My sister and I were so happy to be united, even if for a limited time. Whenever I had spare time after my group activities, I visited Magda and her lovely baby, Ildi, whose Hebrew name was Miriam. She was a beautiful little angel and I had a lot of fun with her and Magda. I was very proud to be an uncle at the mature age of thirteen and a half. Also, Magda cooked all kinds of delicacies that we didn't get in the camp dining room, using the ingredients we were supplied with by the camp or the UNRRA.

After we settled in and the rest of the groups arrived, the maintenance duties of the camp were divided between the different organizations. The kitchen went to the Mizrachi group; transportation and the supply of camp needs came to us in the Hanhac; and all the other responsibilities, such as education, cultural programs, the laundry and so on were taken care of by other groups.

All the different Zionist groups marched to the dining room in military formation, and there was constant competition among the groups. The leaders were always appraising each group's performances, and sports and other forms of competitive activities kept us busy. As time passed and no one could tell how long we would be staying in our camp, classes were organized and shops for learning trades were set up with the appropriate machines and tools. Also, different trips were organized into Germany. The most memorable one was when our Hanhac group organized a get-together for all the groups in Germany at the time. It was held in a camp in Bad Reichenhall, a picturesque town located under mountains with ski lifts and chalets. The camp's parade ground was huge and could accommodate all of us, and we had lots of fun, engaging in all kinds of competitions between the different camps' delegations. The housing consisted of large apartments where the camp population — a few thousand Jews, survivors from different eastern European countries — lived. For the Hanhac get-together, we were accommodated in the buildings' large attics and were supplied with US army cots, blankets and pillows.

Germany was undersupplied with most things, especially food, gasoline and cigarettes, but in the camps, we had a lot of items from the UNRRA, such as light white bread, which the German population didn't have but yearned for; meanwhile, the Germans had heavy dark wheat and grain breads we wanted, so a sort of bartering developed.

The shortage of gas meant that the majority of cars and buses had been converted to run on charcoal. Vehicles were equipped with burners and carried a reserve supply of fuel in bags. When a burner needed additional energy, a driver would put on gloves, take a bag of charcoal off the roof and fill it. Cars fuelled this way drove slower than those with gasoline engines and had especial difficulty on mountainous elevations.

Our trucks from the UNRRA got ample gasoline, so when we went on an organized trip to nearby Berchtesgaden, the site of Hitler's famous Eagle's Nest up on a high mountain, the climb was made slowly but without any difficulty. The road was full of sharp turns where there had been SS checkpoints during the war. When we arrived, the view was breathtaking, but the famous nest itself was a great disappointment. It was a good-sized modern villa, standing alone on the mountaintop, whereas Hitler's house, in nearby Berghof, had been surrounded by similar but somewhat smaller villas built for other leaders of the Third Reich. In Berghof, the few interesting features of the house included an enormous window, which we were told could be electronically worked; in the villa, there was the great party room, which could accommodate many guests. Also, the villa had a brass-lined elevator that could transport fifty-three people.

Next, the whole group from Aschau went to nearby Lake Königssee, nestled between two very high mountains. On two sides of the lake were sheer stone walls coming out of the water. Königssee had only three points of approach, the first being the harbour full of tourist boats, one of which we boarded. As we reached a certain point, the captain sounded a few notes on a musical instrument, which came back to us in the form of hundreds of echoes. It was an experience not to be forgotten. Shortly after this musical experience, we let some passengers disembark at a convent and continued to an island on the lake's farthest point. We left the boat and went by foot toward a smaller lake, Obersee. It was about three to four kilometres from the harbour.

When we arrived there, it was lunchtime, so some of us started to prepare our lunch with supplies brought from camp. As preparation would take some time, some of the guys went to try their climbing skills. To the untrained eye, the slopes didn't look difficult, but they were; nonetheless, the climbers reached a decent height. But it wasn't until our climbers tried to turn around and descend that they realized that the unstable slope, which had not been too difficult to climb, would be very difficult to descend. They shouted down to us for help. We had to organize layers of protective rings so they could make their way down slowly, step by step. It took quite a while but finally, every one of us was down and safe.

Back in Bad Reichenhall lived my first cousin and her husband, so for me it was a double enjoyment to be there. On the way back to Aschau, after our jamboree ended, we stopped in another interesting place, Schloss Herrenchiemsee. This palace, situated on an island, was so beautiful that later in life I took all my family to see and enjoy it. The island was purchased by King Ludwig II of Bavaria for his personal use, and he started to build a palace there. The story goes that he spent only a few days there before he drowned, and construction of the palace was never completed. Visitors take a boat to the island from the city of Prien and then can walk to the palace or ride in a horse-drawn buggy to the entrance. To describe the magnificent structure, I would need a good few pages. Only one floor is open to visitors, but even on that floor, one room has never been finished. According to our guide, no government wanted to spend the huge amount of money it would take to finish the room in the style of the rest of the complex. I have visited many European castles, but none has come close to that one.

Back at Aschau, we returned to our routine. By now, many months had passed, in which we often got letters from family and friends in Hungary. Some friends from Hanhac indicated that Aliyah Bet was now going to Palestine from Hungary. Meanwhile, we heard that we were likely to be stuck in Aschau for a long time, because the Jewish authorities were using the large number of refugees as bargaining chips in the fight for an independent Jewish state. Around December 1946, I decided to leave with my friend Garzo and another friend and return to Hungary, where we felt we would have a better chance for aliyah. It was not an easy departure. My cousin Yehuda tried especially hard to convince us to stay, but we were three stubborn individuals.[5] My sister Magda also tried to convince me to stay, but she well knew that when I made my mind up, it was final.

---

5   The entire Hanhac group led by Yehuda ended up on the *Exodus*, a ship that was carrying 4,500 Jewish refugees from Europe to British Mandate Palestine in July 1947. In an incident that focused public attention on the plight of European Jews who wished to settle in British Mandate Palestine, British troops prevented the ship from landing and the Jewish refugees were forcibly returned to Displaced Persons camps in Europe. The majority of the refugees eventually settled in Israel after the state was declared.

Our Journey

We said our goodbyes and set out to the local railway station, intending to travel to a larger station where we could find a train going toward Hungary. Luckily, we were able to join a train right at the local station. It was carrying Hungarian soldiers who had been held as prisoners of war and released and was going directly to Hungary. On my arrival in Budapest, my mother welcomed me ecstatically and with great relief, even though she was resigned to the idea of my going to Israel. She still hoped to join me and my sister Magda one day; shortly after I had left, Magda arrived in the Holy Land with both her husband, who she had reunited with, and their baby.

While I was away, my other sister, Edith, got married to a farmer by the name of Martin. He had lost his wife and two children in the war, and after liberation, he had returned to his village and was able to reclaim his family's properties in houses and substantial tracts of land. The Grofs had arranged this marriage for Edith, their adopted daughter, and in their eyes, it would be a good, solid marriage. Edith was in her new home in the village of Baktalórántháza. Martin leased his lands to the richest farmer of the village, who worked the land and split the income with him. Martin had also become a wholesaler of potatoes, coal, firewood and petrol for the tractors.

As the Communist Party's influence grew, especially in institutions where large workers' group were unionized, the union bosses organized purchases of commodities in volumes that offered savings to their members. The union of railway workers was one of the strongest in Hungary and represented hundreds of thousands of workers. My brother-in-law Martin was approached to supply a number of railway carts of potatoes to be divided among any union members who wanted to participate and paid a deposit.

However, a problem arose after the contract was signed by the head of the railway workers' union; he was an old-guard fascist turned communist, who decided to fix the supplier, the "dirty Jew." He directed the whole train with the potatoes to a sidetrack and ordered it to be unloaded into one huge pile. In a few days, a part of this huge pile started to rot. Then he went to court and demanded Martin be arrested under charges that he had cheated the railway union members by selling them rotten potatoes.

This all happened right when I arrived. Martin was taken to jail in Budapest, where he was awaiting the outcome of the trial. Of course, my sister Edith came to Budapest to help out in any way she could. Edith asked me if I was willing to go to their house in the village until this crazy thing was over. They didn't want to leave their sizable house with their maid and her brother who worked general jobs around the house and drove their horse-drawn buggy. I agreed to go and had a chance while there to learn horseback riding, which was to my liking. I had an easy life in the house and the village, where my brother-in-law was an important individual and well respected. I was seen as a young gentleman from the capital city.

Meanwhile, I got a daily phone call reporting on what was happening in court. The case became of general interest for the legal establishment in Budapest. Anyone who was following the case soon realized that there was nothing that the court could do legally against Martin, as his contract stipulated that the potatoes were to be inspected at the station where they were loaded.

One evening's report described a very ugly miscarriage of justice by the communist union. Edith told me that a delegation of union members appeared in court and in a noisy fashion declared to the judge that if the accused rich guy didn't get satisfactory punishment, they would carry out his punishment themselves. After this declaration, they went out to the courtyard where a hanging platform was displayed, and they mockingly performed the act of lynching. The judge immediately ordered a significant detachment of police to stand guard and prevent violence, but after the lunch break, the judge's verdict included every possible punishment on the books: first, ten years in jail, then twenty years of prohibition against working at his previous trade, twenty years of exile from his current address, a fine of one million and other smaller punishments. The union delegates felt satisfied and dispersed.

The judge knew that he had no case against Martin, but it looked like he had to placate these hotheaded thugs. So Martin became an example — punishments like his would become common later under the full communist regime. The only concession that the judge made in Martin's favour was letting him off mandatory jail time. At night, Martin was released and advised to stay away from his home for quite a while. Edith came back to the village and looked after Martin's business.

After the court business died down and Edith returned home, I went back to Budapest. It was February 1947, the middle of the school year. To join in would have been difficult and besides, I didn't know how long it would be before I would be leaving on my way to Palestine. My mother and I decided — given that I was the only surviving male member of our family — I would become the breadwinner. I needed to learn some kind of trade to achieve that goal. It didn't matter which one, since when my chance to go arrived, I would be able to take advantage of whatever experience I'd gained and build on it later. The only problem was that in Hungary in those days, one's guardian had to pay an annual fee for the first two years of any apprenticeship program in case the apprentice proved to be unproductive. In addition, the newest apprentice got all the dirtiest jobs. He had to keep the shop clean, and at snack and lunchtime he had to bring everyone's orders from the market.

When I began my own apprenticeship as a machinist, I was given a piece of steel and a file and instructed to file about half an inch off to make one side of the metal straight and smooth. As time progressed, I had to work with odd shapes or fit pieces into round, square or other shaped holes. To work on the machines at that time was only a dream. My shop, though similar to thousands of others, was a very basic one. It was situated on the second floor of an apartment building, occupying what had probably been two separate apartments. We had milling machines, drills, sanders and other necessary equipment. The whole operation ran on a single large motor, which drove one long shaft the full length of the ceiling. On the shaft were wheels for each machine with three steps for the different speeds required. A long stick with a small rod coming out of it was used to switch the bolts from level to level as needed. You had to be careful not to put the rod on at the wrong angle as it could twist the handle and injure you.

It wasn't the ideal apprenticeship, given how primitive the shop was, but anyone who learned a trade there would be an excellent machinist. In addition to the work itself, apprentices had to be registered and participate in an apprentice school program two or three times weekly after lunch. This program not only supplied the theoretical part of the job, but it also gave me an opportunity to connect with my Zionist group. The regular routine called for three weekly activities: first, the meeting of the *kvutza*; second, the Saturday *kein* meeting for all the *kvutzot*; and third, the customary Sunday trip to the Buda Mountains or, in case of rain, to the national pool complex on Margaret Island. Some of us, including me, added a fourth activity: the creation of a four-voice choir with a total of sixty participants. As I loved singing, I enjoyed choir days. We became so good that we had concerts in the Music Academy concert hall, also known as the Liszt Ferenc Academy of Music. This went on quite a long time, until the communists forbade it, concerned that we were sending messages against their communist teachings to such large audiences.

~

As time passed in 1947 and 1948 without any possibility of moving on, many of us in the Hanhac group became quite restless. Meanwhile, though, a small group of about fifteen of us became very close-knit, and some even evolved into couples. My friendship with one girl, Kati, developed into a full-fledged love affair, which was eventually accepted by both families. Kati's family was wealthy, unlike mine, but I never felt that our different backgrounds were an obstacle to our relationship. This is not to say that I was not envious sometimes when I met with Kati's high school friends and recognized in them the education and culture I'd had no chance to acquire myself. But Kati herself never let me feel this inadequacy. Whenever we had a chance to be together, we had a wonderful time.

On May 14, 1948, when David Ben-Gurion declared the state of Israel a homeland for the Jewish people, we had only muted celebrations because the Communist Party prohibited the existence of Zionist organizations. Therefore, all our activities had to be hidden. Most meetings were held in someone's apartment except for the big Saturday one, which needed a large hall, and it would be rented under another organization's name.

Although the state of Israel now existed, getting there from Hungary was another matter — the communist regime did not easily allow for exit visas, and leaving without one was illegal. The Hanhac members planning to make aliyah, therefore, were instructed in how to prepare for such a clandestine trip. We were told to dress in the same kind of clothing we would wear to visit relatives and to pack two extra belts in a suitcase to be able to carry it like a backpack in case we had to run across fields or other difficult territory. No one was able to tell any of us whether such an event would actually take place, so that no one would be able to implicate anyone in case the authorities got wind of our plans. The only thing we knew was who would pair up with whom for the journey, and that once the signal was given, departure would take place the next day. We, and all our families, went through a tough time waiting, uncertain of what would happen for many long months.

Our *kvutza* leader was a girl named Eka. An excellent leader and friend, she was an engineering student only a few years older than her troopers. We knew that she was involved in smuggling members of our organization across western borders to other countries, and from there to Israel. One Saturday in mid-April of 1949, we went to Eka's apartment after the *kein* meeting to sing and dance. We had been there for a good hour and a half when Eka approached Kati and me to tell us that we were to leave on our aliyah the next day. I wanted to kiss Eka and also to give her hell for waiting so long to notify us about our departure. Eka didn't give us any additional information, such as what time we needed to be at the station or what our destination was. The only thing she told us was that she would come to my apartment around 11:00 a.m. with further instructions, and that no family members would be allowed to accompany us to the station.

All this mysterious structure was to avoid any leaks that could jeopardize our friends. I was told that when we got to the border, we would be among other couples travelling as individuals who, like us, would all be united there. Then we would meet some smugglers who would guide us through the safe fields to the other side, where two taxis would be waiting to bring us to a city for further transfer on our route. I was appointed to be the group leader and was given a substantial amount of money to pay the first group of smugglers after they brought us to the meeting place with the taxis. The fees for the taxis would be paid by the Zionist underground in the town that was to be our destination.

We waited anxiously at my house. Eleven o'clock passed, 11:15 a.m. passed, and finally around 11:30 a.m. Eka arrived breathlessly with the information that our train would be leaving from the eastern railway station close to my home at 2:00 p.m. She didn't tell us where we were going or what tickets to buy but assured us that she would meet us near the ticket office. Kati went home by taxi to say her goodbyes and to pick up her suitcase and hand luggage and then returned to my home so we could go to the railway station together. When we arrived at the giant departure hall and looked around, we saw a number of friendly faces in other little groups. I also saw my mother at a distance, saying her silent goodbyes.

It was almost 1:40 p.m. when Eka finally appeared and told us which city we were going to so that we could buy the tickets, but she didn't tell us who would be leading the trip. Just as the train was about to depart, Eka ran up to tell us that on arrival at our destination we should find a fellow with a large checkered coat and follow him. Also, as a last-minute instruction, she reminded us not to talk to the other couples and if anyone asked us questions, we were to tell them we were going to visit relatives. Then she wished us a successful trip.

After we'd settled into our section and stored our luggage on the racks, we went out to stand by the window to see familiar places fly by. After a time, a young gentleman approached us to enquire about our group. We were surprised and told him that he was mistaken, as we didn't belong to one; we were just going to visit relatives. He asked us a few times in different ways and received the same answer. This frustrated him, so he finally gave up and left us alone. Another couple from our organization that stood not too far from us saw the exchange with this mysterious fellow and asked us why the group leader had talked to us, and why he left in such an irritated state. We told them that we hadn't admitted that we belonged to a group, as all we knew from Eka was that a guy in a large checkered coat would be taking us to our first meeting place with the smugglers. They replied that this was our guy; he'd just left his checkered jacket hanging in his compartment.

Six couples from different compartments followed the man with the checkered coat off the train. Until we got to our destination, it was pitch dark. He led us to the back entrance of a pub, where we stored our luggage. As we ate sausage sandwiches made of tasty dark farmer's bread, peppers and cucumbers and had something to drink, we were told that the smuggler would be arriving later. We said good-bye to our checkered-coat friend, who wished us a successful crossing into Czechoslovakia. Czechoslovakia was also a communist country, so we knew that we had to avoid patrols, as they would put us in jail and probably transport us back to Hungary where the option would also be jail, unless the local Aliyah Bet paid a large price per person for our release.

Finally, our friendly smuggler came. Everyone fixed the suitcases with belts to their backs. The smuggler warned us that it would be a hard crossing through potato fields in pitch darkness. Before starting, he wanted to see the money he would receive on our arrival. I showed him the agreed-upon amount. After a few hours of hard marching, we were on the Czechoslovakian side of the border, where our smuggler left us in an abandoned barn close to a highway. He told us that when dawn came, the highway would be visible and we would see two taxis coming to transport us to the city of Košice (called Kassa in Hungarian).

As the first light dawned, two taxis arrived and we happily approached them with our luggage. One of the drivers started speaking Hungarian, and I approached him to find out what he wanted. I was shocked when he demanded full payment for the trip. I explained to him that my instructions indicated that he would be paid on our arrival by the Zionist underground. He started to laugh and said that the Zionist office had no money left as they had spent a fortune to free people who had been jailed after being caught when they tried to enter Czechoslovakia. I told him that I had received only what I'd paid to the smuggler who brought us to our meeting place. We didn't have any more money, because we had been warned that if we got caught with money we could be accused of foreign money smuggling, adding another crime to our illegal entry. He wanted to leave us, as he had previously taken a group without payment, but I pleaded with him, saying that if he left us on the highway, sooner or later we would be captured by a patrol. I suggested that I could convince my group to deposit their valuables — watches, rings, gold chains and even our luggage — with him until he was paid. He resisted until our pleas and tears softened him and we loaded the taxis and set out for Košice.

A patrol car stopped us on our way there. The policemen and the driver had a loud discussion until the driver paid a bunch of money to the police and we continued on. This little affair added to the payment we'd already promised, a few thousand Czech korunas to be paid on arrival. At the transit camp, the driver told us to unload the luggage and asked that I go with him to the office to get his money. His concerns proved to be right; the guy in the office had no money. The driver started to swear at me and the others, but nothing helped. Finally, he declared he would no longer pick up new arrivals as he was being cheated out of his fee. He had our valuables, but according to him, they only covered a small portion of the money he should have received. I felt lousy because I knew that in Hungary the organization had ample funds, but they had stopped us from taking any of it.

We spent one night in a transfer camp and were told that the next day we would go on to another Czech town, Bratislava (Pozsony in Hungarian), where we would stay for a while. Our camp was formerly a Jewish school and was not the most comfortable place. Soon after our arrival in Pozsony, Kati's sister, Zsuzsi, and her husband arrived, having been smuggled in a similar fashion by our Hanhac group. They joined us in our large bedroom.

As the food in the camp was unsatisfactory, we went into the town to find some decent food at inexpensive restaurants. This area of Czechoslovakia had belonged to Hungary until 1918, the end of World War I. As Hungary fought on the losing side with the Germans, the victorious nations had cut away two-thirds of Hungary and given it to Czechoslovakia, Romania (Transylvania) and Yugoslavia, but the population continued to speak and be educated in Hungarian as well as the other local languages. For this reason, in Kassa and in Pozsony, most of the people spoke Hungarian and cooked Hungarian food, so it was easy to find places that offered us dishes we were used to eating.

The main problem was coming up with enough money for these outings. Luckily, a few of us had hidden some bills in well-protected places. The second problem was the danger of being caught by the authorities. During one of our restaurant visits, six or eight of us sitting in a nice little place were being quite noisy. After we ordered our dishes, we noticed a guy sitting alone, dressed like an official or a detective, watching us. We started to worry about whether he might cause us serious problems. As each of us got his or her dishes, we rushed to finish them, hoping to get out before he could call the police or other authorities. When we asked for our bill, the waiter said it had been paid already. This increased our anxiety. We rushed out, but nothing bad happened.

A few years later, Eve, one of the girls from our group, happened to recognize this guy in Israel. She told him we had thought that he was a detective and what a scare he had created for us. He apologized and explained that, as a friendly gesture, he had paid our bill in the knowledge that guys like us had only limited funds. Eve thanked him on our behalf.

We stayed in Pozsony (Bratislava) for three weeks. At the gate of our camp, a guard was always posted. The poor fellow had to sit all day at his post, sweating in his uniform. Meanwhile, we were constantly going to the city, as there was very little to do in the camp. A few of us usually went together — Kati and I, her sister and brother-in-law, and sometimes more from our group. We explored the beautiful city's most interesting parts. All in all, we had a ball, as most of us were couples and we enjoyed each other's company very much.

We kept imagining our ultimate dream of arrival in Israel, now an independent Jewish country, a country that had fought for survival from the first day of its existence. From the news we received, we knew that immediately upon Ben-Gurion's declaration of Israel, the Palestinian Arabs had joined with surrounding Arab countries and attacked Israel. Syria, Jordan, Egypt, Lebanon and Iraq dispatched military units and Israel defended itself with its tiny ill-equipped force. Yet, this tiny army saved the country, making it a destination for Jewish refugees from around the world, including Holocaust survivors from Europe like us, as well as hundreds of thousands of Jews who fled from many Arab countries after the 1948 War of Independence.

Unbelievable effort and determination was needed to accommodate such a huge influx of newcomers. Beside Israeli society's own sacrifice and effort, the free world's Jewish communities extended help and assistance to enable Israel to absorb such large waves of *olim*, immigrants. Now we were on our way to fulfill the same dream, doing our part to strengthen the country for a better future.

Kati's parents' confidence that I would be able to protect and support her on our journey, and also once we arrived in Israel, had influenced them to let her leave Hungary with me, even though we were only sixteen years old at the time. Kati's parents and my mother became quite close, so much so that when, after our departure from Budapest, Kati's father was arrested and jailed just because he was a wealthy mattress manufacturer, Kati's mother moved in with my mother so that neither of them would have to be alone.

After close to three weeks in Bratislava, we were told to be ready for our next destination, which was to be Vienna, Austria. We were warned that we would have to pass through Czechoslovakia's customs, which checked rigorously for items deemed to be forbidden to take out of the country. First among these was money, whether local or foreign currency; next was all merchandise purchased in Czechoslovakia itself. As many of us had such items, the tension was high. I mentioned earlier that before our departure from Budapest we were warned not to take any money with us so as to avoid being accused of smuggling foreign currency, which was a serious offense.

Nonetheless, most of us eventually admitted to each other that our parents had hidden some extra money in our luggage. The inventiveness they used in finding safe places to hide cash was amazing. In my case, my mother relied on the assistance of one of my good friends from the first days of my entry into Hanhac, Mordechai Kraemer Morgo. His family lived down the block and ran a business manufacturing men's belts and suspenders in their apartment. When our time for departure got closer, they suggested that they produce a belt connected to a pair of suspenders by three leather triangles, which would make good hiding places for a few bills. A fourth triangle was placed on the belt itself. My mother provided four hundred-dollar bills, which were then sewn into these invisible pockets. This was a substantial fortune for me as a teenager.

Besides the money sewn into my belt, I had a small plastic-covered roll of smaller bills for urgent needs. This was pushed inside a toothpaste tube. As we progressed through the hall toward the customs officers, we slid our suitcases onto long metal tables. I noticed the customs officer squeezing the toothpaste tube of the people in front of me, judging their reactions to see who was nervous and might be hiding something. So when I got closer, I poked my hand into my suitcase and moved a brown box that was a sewing kit to another location. When the time came to search my belongings, the customs guy went superficially through the contents of the suitcase before suddenly grabbing the little sewing box. With a victorious smile, he opened the box and emptied it onto the table. Seeing the box's contents and my surprised expression, he ordered me to collect everything and move down the line quickly. This little victory made me feel proud. I think that requiring street smarts to survive in an underground organization from such an early age provided me with an extraordinary sense of observation as well as the capacity to use it in different circumstances.

After passing through customs, we were ushered into waiting buses from the Austrian side. They were spacious, clean and really elegant. Immediately, we could see a great difference between communist services and those provided by the other Western countries.

Our next stop was Vienna. After World War ii, Vienna was divided into four districts, each governed by one of the victorious Allies: American, British, French and Soviet. The MP (military police) jeeps carried soldiers from each of the four powers into each of the districts. Upon our arrival, we were warned not to enter or even get too close to the Soviet district, where unsuspecting visitors had previously disappeared.

Again, a former hospital, on Auerspergstrasse, served as our camp. The accommodations were very nice, and since we were situated not too far from the city centre, we were free to roam around and explore as much as we wished, as long as we adhered to the warnings regarding the Soviets. Here, again, our stay dragged on for weeks.

My mother sent me a letter saying that relatives of ours would be arriving in Vienna soon on their way to Israel, so maybe we could meet them. Their names were László and Olga Szekulesz. László was a major figure on the Zionist scene, and after the war, he was one of the leaders of the National Jewish Relief Committee in Hungary. As the communist regime became more and more restrictive, the Szekuleszes decided to move to Israel. He applied to the proper authorities and got one of the rare visas with a permit to take their belongings in a large container. This almost never happened. The Szekuleszes were quite wealthy before the war and they were able to hide a good part of their wealth among their belongings, which were being shipped to an apartment on Mount Carmel, in Haifa, which they had been able to purchase while still in Hungary.

Our meeting in Vienna was pleasant, and it was interesting to meet such an important relative in this city so distant from home. But our meeting was quite short, because the Szekuleszes were notified by the authorities that they should leave their hotel as soon as possible; they were staying too close to the Soviet sector and the Soviets were looking for them in order to send them back to Hungary.

We kissed and wished them the best of luck, promising to look them up in Haifa.

Another thing that happened during our stay in Vienna was my seventeenth birthday on May 19. We celebrated in a beautiful *conditoria* (cake-and-coffee place). Knowing my craving for almonds, Kati found a store not far from our camp and bought a sizable bag for me. I was really delighted by the thoughtfulness of this gesture, which showed her love for me. The bag lasted quite a while, although all the gang shared in my present.

At the end of three weeks, we were notified to get ready to move again, just like in Bratislava. This time we went to the Salzburg transit camp. A former military camp with limited facilities, this place was not as comfortable as our accommodations in Vienna had been. But we had total freedom to roam around Salzburg, the amazing birthplace of Mozart. There were so many things to see and do that our pleasure overshadowed the relative discomfort of the camp, and even there, we had lots of fun with our gang. We had discussions about Zionism and the recent war, and we sang and danced often. We learned newer songs coming out of Israel or other music from camp survivors.

The newly created leadership organized many different trips within Austria as well as to nearby tourist attractions. We also took long walks into mountainous areas around the city and had picnics. In short, besides missing our families and our continuing anxiety about getting to our final destination, we didn't suffer any hardship. And the company of our girlfriends and boyfriends, as well as the general company of the group, was some compensation for the homesickness.

As had already become routine, three weeks after our arrival in Salzburg came the news that we would be continuing our journey again. Our next destination was going to be the town of Trani in southern Italy. We made our journey there by train. The views along the way were quite different from Czechoslovakia or Austria, since a good part of our voyage followed the shore of the Mediterranean, which most, if not all of us, were seeing for the first time in our lives. The scenery slowly changed from a mountainous to a flat horizon and from familiar trees and vegetation to palm trees and beautiful beaches.

At Trani's railway station, American military trucks appeared like magic to transport us to the camp. This was an Italian military camp with the customary long barracks. Everything was an ugly sand colour — the buildings, the roads, the soil — except the vegetation, including the palm trees and cacti that lined most of Trani's main streets. The influence of a few hundred years of Moorish occupation was obvious everywhere. Churches' turrets as well as public buildings showed a substantial Middle Eastern influence; for example, many of the windows and doors of the larger buildings had rounded tops. The biggest surprise came when I realized that a vendor pushing his cart full of a colourful variety of fruits was singing a melody that sounded totally Arabic.

Shortly after our arrival, we found out where the public beaches were so we could swim in the glorious blue Mediterranean. We had the good fortune of avoiding the usual language barrier since Kati's sister, Zsuzsi, was a graduate of an Italian school in Budapest and had taken additional courses to teach Italian. Given this good fortune, we had no difficulty communicating with the locals we met daily on the beach. Hardly any spoke a language other than Italian.

There was not too much to see or do in this town, apart from going to the sea or taking a stroll on the pedestrian mall along the waterfront. This tree-lined walkway had a lineup of ice-cream and espresso shops that offered lots of sweet selections. When the temperature dropped somewhat in the afternoons, most of the youngsters of the town gathered there. It was striking to see that most showed up with fancy sweaters draped over their shoulders and dragged with them very fancy bicycles. Having been a cyclist myself since the age of seven, it was a real pleasure to see so many variations, some of which I assumed were custom-made.

Now, we knew that when our three weeks in Trani were over, we would go to Bari, a nearby port from which a boat would take us to our ultimate destination, Israel. During the many weeks of our journey, we had continued taking Hebrew lessons, so at least we would be able to converse a little when we finally arrived. Our long journey took three months. I imagine that the logistics of moving all the candidates for aliyah took some serious planning and preparation in Europe as well as in Israel, where all the newcomers had to be directed to suitable places to start their new lives.

When three weeks had passed, we prepared to go to Bari. On arrival, we found a ship waiting for us in port. The name of the ship was *Atzmaut*, Independence in Hebrew; it was a converted cargo ship that could carry close to 4,500 passengers. People continued to arrive from many directions to make this historic trip with us. Each arriving group was assigned a specific area for the trip. Our group got bunkbeds crowded together in almost the lowest level of the vessel. The new Israeli authorities didn't have the luxury to transport the potential newcomers in great comfort, but we idealistic Zionist youth didn't have any special expectations for the last leg of our journey. We just wanted to arrive.

As soon as we got our beds arranged, we started to feel the rough motions of the sea, even though the ship was still in port. The sick feeling in our stomachs prompted us to explore the ship to see if we could find more favourable accommodations. Kati and I roamed around all the levels, but we couldn't see any better solutions. So we went onto the main deck, where we saw the lifeboats hanging over the side of the ship on their hoists. Under them was ample space with no burning sun and with lots of fresh air. We decided this would be an ideal place for the trip. So Kati stayed on guard to make sure nobody else stole our genius idea before I was able to bring some blankets and pillows to create a shelter for us. I made a number of trips carrying the necessary items, including a mattress from one of the bunkbeds. We only hoped that no one from the crew would force us out of these super accommodations. Luckily that didn't happen. The only time we came out of our exclusive spot was to get food or use the services.

After all the passengers were loaded, the preparations started for departure. The whole boat burst out into song to celebrate this great event. Under glorious sunshine, we said our goodbyes to Europe, the place that had provided us with both the best and the worst experiences of our young lives — wonderful childhood memories, but also horrors we couldn't escape but simply had to endure. To survive hell, we found solace in the dream of creating a Jewish homeland where, even if hard times might await us, we would be among our own people, people who wouldn't try to kill or torture us just for being Jews.

Despite all the fond memories I had of good times, I also felt tremendous anger and hatred for my former countrymen. Hungary was a Catholic country that was supposed to be full of God-fearing people. How could they have sunk so abominably low as to kill those neighbours, friends and partners who had worked with them in harmony? In the record time of six weeks, Hungary deported over 440,000 Jews to concentration camps, where most perished. They did this when most people knew the war was already lost, and when one might have expected them to concentrate on protecting their country against the invading enemy. Instead, they employed hundreds of railway cars and thousands of police and soldiers to ensure the deaths of men, women and children whose only crime was their religion. Having lost my dear father and two brothers and over a hundred members of my close family, I didn't feel too much regret leaving the continent that for us Jews had become a huge cemetery.

I am fully aware that there were exceptions, that some people helped Jews to survive and, in the process, endangered their own lives and those of their families. They have the eternal gratitude of the Jewish people. But this memoir is my indictment against the majority of Europeans for the crimes they committed against the Jews. Most of us wanted to contribute to the best of our abilities in our respective fields of endeavour for the betterment of whichever country we resided in. Certainly, in Hungary, as I'm sure was similar in other European countries, the Jewish contribution in all fields was disproportionate to their numbers and enriched not only national but international life.

The Hope

Our ship made steady progress and finally, early one morning, we heard that soon we would be able to see the shoreline of Israel, specifically the port of Haifa, where we would be arriving. It seemed like all the ship's passengers lined up for this exceptional event. Most of us stood close to the rails to witness this miracle with wet eyes. The most memorable Hebrew songs filled the morning air and as we reached the pier, everyone burst out with "Hatikvah" (The Hope), the hymn of Israel.

At the gangway, people with signs waited for each group to follow them after the official formalities had been performed. Everyone welcomed us with the customary greeting *baruch haba*, blessed be the one who comes, followed by food and drink. Then each group went to the bus that would take them to their destination. Some were taken to different kibbutzim; young people who came without families, like us, were driven to various residential institutions run by an agency called Aliyat Hano'ar, Youth Aliyah. These youth institutions, called *mossads*, were built close to kibbutzim so that we could attend school as well as provide extra labour harvesting fruits and vegetables.

The Youth Aliyah dealt with children from early school age up to age sixteen. Our group of twenty-two Hungarian youth were mostly older than sixteen, but in our case an exception was made so that we could help establish a new institution before it was time for us to go into the army. Our *mossad* was called Neve Hadassah. It was adjacent to Kibbutz Tel Yitzhak, so we were welcomed officially by a member of the kibbutz who was also the director of Neve Hadassah. The *mossad* was not quite ready to receive us as the first youth group, so we lived in tents on the kibbutz. We walked there every morning to work on different projects, such as completion of the water lines and the sewer system, under the supervision of established kibbutz members.

Not too long after our arrival, Neve Hadassah was able to receive us fully. We left the tents on the kibbutz and moved into new housing units that became our homes for a while. We had two directors; one, Yitzchak Barkai, oversaw the management of the nearby kibbutz. The director of the school, Moshe Sadmi, was closest to us. He and his wife, Genia, were two extremely talented, dedicated and lovely people. In order to expedite our schooling in Hebrew, Moshe didn't allow us any Hungarian communication, going so far as to take away Hungarian books or other written materials. This draconian step was not very popular among us but a year later, when most of us faced army induction, we realized how it had helped our integration into Israeli society. For Kati and myself, as well as for a few other serious couples, another difficult adjustment was that our new living arrangements interfered with our close relations as lovers. Over our three-month journey, we had lived as an official couple, but the new reality didn't permit this. Of course, this didn't dampen our feelings for each other.

One of the major events of the opening of Neve Hadassah was going to be a concert of the *mossad* choir. We had an excellent conductor who lived in a little settlement close by, so it was easy for him to come to us, sometimes more than once a day. The time from the announcement of this concert to the date of the performance was quite short, and we knew that a large audience would attend: friends and relatives of the kids in our own *mossad*; members from other kibbutzim; representatives of various government offices; delegations of other *mossads* from our party of Hanoar Hatzioni; and also delegations from other institutions, including the leadership and guests of Hadassah, which we were connected to, as our name indicated. So the event had to be well prepared for, and refreshments provided for a great many visitors. Organizing all of the above was added to our normal daily school and other activities.

Preparation for the official opening went on feverishly. Then one day we got disturbing news about our choirmaster — the poor man had been involved in a car accident and, badly hurt, would need a long time to recuperate. When he returned from his hospital stay, I went to see him and he told me that he wanted me to take his place. This request was both flattering and scary. I tried to convince him that I wouldn't be able to do the job, but he was adamant that with his guidance, I would do just fine. I had mentioned earlier that I sang in our synagogue choir before the Holocaust and had been part of the Hanhac choir, like many of our Hungarian aliyah group. Still, I had never learned music formally and couldn't even read it. Nonetheless, having worked with us, our choirmaster felt that I had the ability to lead the choir.

At first, my friends didn't take me seriously, but the choirmaster came in a wheelchair a few times, and with his assistance, things started to fall in place and the rehearsals improved. When opening day arrived, I felt nervous but confident that our choir would perform well. And that is exactly what happened. The general director introduced the choir and explained how I came to be the conductor. Our choirmaster sat in the first row, providing encouragement. We got ovations for every song and the leadership of our *mossad* got great reviews.

Our kitchen staff, teachers and trainers gave our guests a memorable day. This took place in 1950, only two years after Israel's War of Independence. In the midst of handling such an influx of new *olim*, times were very hard. Nothing was in abundance. Certain food items were rationed and even fruit that the country produced was hard to come by and was reserved for export. Still, for the opening ceremonies, we were able to treat our guests to a feast fit, if not for a king, for lower aristocracy.

~

Most of our group who had arrived in Israel at seventeen years of age in 1949 reached the age for entering the army in 1950. Knowing how soon we would have this responsibility, the Aliyat Hano'ar had purposely brought us to Neve Hadassah to establish basic skills for the army and for civilian life afterwards. One of the things I did was get a driver's licence. My maintenance manager gave me driving lessons in preparation for the test, which I passed in Hadera, a city north of the *mossad*. On our way back home, he let me drive for the first time on one of the main roads in Israel. This was the main artery between Haifa and Tel Aviv at that time (later a parallel road was built close to the seashore). I felt very proud that I would be entering the army soon as an official driver.

Then two things happened to change my plans. From an early age, I'd had a hernia that hadn't bothered me too much. But in the *mossad*, my job required me to carry heavy boxes of produce. The maintenance manager and I went to Netanya weekly to obtain supplies from the Tnuva milk and produce cooperative warehouses. Lifting those heavy boxes, I started to feel pain in the hernia area. Our doctor suggested I undergo an operation to fix it prior to my military induction. An appointment was made for me at the hospital in Nahariya, in the northern part of Israel. It was quite a lengthy operation of three and a half hours, but I was without any anxiety and, under local anesthesia, fully aware of everything the whole time, watching the operation on the ceiling mirrors. I was even able to joke with the doctor and his crew and then walk from the operating room to the recovery room with a nurse's help. In a few short days, I was discharged and picked up to return to the *mossad*, where I was directed to take it easy for a few weeks.

In front of our rooms, we had tried to create some small gardens from the barren grounds. To protect our efforts, they were enclosed by a thin wire strung between sticks. One day during my recuperation, I went outside to welcome a visitor and, not noticing the low wire, I tripped and broke my left ankle. Once again, I had to visit a hospital, this time to get a walking cast put on. Now that I had broken my ankle, things changed for me drastically. My entire group had to go to the army, and I had been counting on being with some of my friends when conscripted, but this was not to be. Even the younger girls like Kati were leaving to go to nursing school at the Rothschild Hospital in Haifa. I was the only one who could not go on to the next stage of my life.

Before she left, a very painful thing happened between Kati and me, mostly because of my own stupidity. We both had a few friends and relations to visit when we had free time. I had my sister Magda and her two children, Miriam and David, as well as my cousins Shlomo in Ramat Gan, Moshe in Petah Tikva, Yehuda (the leader of Hanoar Hatzioni, who had brought me out of Hungary in January 1946), who was in a kibbutz called Yehi'am in the upper Galilee, and one other cousin in Kibbutz Ramat HaShofet. In addition, Olga and her husband, Laci, who we had met in Vienna, lived in Haifa. Out of all these relatives, we most often visited Moshe and his wife, Vally, with their children, Yehuda and, of course, my sister Magda. Kati had only her sister, Zsuzsi, and her brother-in-law, Gordon, and a German family who were friends of Kati's family and also lived in Haifa.

Kati's sister and her husband were doing well. Soon after their arrival, they both got jobs, he as an engineer and she as a teacher of Italian. Both earned relatively good incomes and lived in government-supplied housing in a newcomers' camp. But my sister Magda was in a terrible situation. When they arrived from Germany, she and her husband settled in a house that had only two rooms, back to back, with no windows. My sister's husband, Engel, assigned her and their two children to one of the rooms and moved to the second room with a new girlfriend. I tried to help her as best I could but since I was still in the *mossad*, the only money I had was that given to me by Olga and Laci and my cousin Moshe. It was not much, but it still helped my sister and her kids. My family was very close. Even though my parents weren't wealthy, they still managed to help any relative in need. That's what I learned from them and how I tried to live.

Unfortunately, Kati's brother-in-law, Gordon, who I found quite selfish, didn't like me doing this and voiced his displeasure angrily. That got me boiling mad. But it seemed to me that Kati didn't fully support my position, so I became disillusioned and decided to break up with her. It was a difficult decision, as I loved Kati very much, but I couldn't see myself joining a family without such compassion. It was a shock to both families back in Hungary because everyone had taken for granted that Kati and I were going to get married. It was equally shocking to Kati and me. But we were very young and made a fateful decision in the heat of the moment.

When the guys from my age group went off to the army and the girls from Kati's to the nursing school, I was left behind in the *mossad*. I became the assistant maintenance man, my status changing from student to employee of the institution. I got a private room, some income and a decent amount of fun. As the assistant maintenance manager, I had the new green Willys jeep for my personal use. Each week, the *mossad's* laundry was transported to a dry-cleaning place in Netanya. To get out to the highway, I had to drive through the kibbutz and pass a spot where hitchhikers stood. After a while, I had some steady female riders, sometimes young girls and sometimes more mature women. The number of women teachers at the *mossad* had also increased, so for a fairly good-looking guy with a private room, it was not difficult to find company. This helped me to forget the loss of Kati. And she and I were still close friends despite the understanding that we would never get married. She continued to keep in contact by letter, inviting me to visit her in Haifa and even visiting me from time to time back at the *mossad*. Once she brought a couple of our old friends from the *mossad* back with her, and it was a very enjoyable weekend as it brought back the heyday of our *mossad* life.

Finally, my own time arrived to go into the army. I said goodbye to all my friends and coworkers and went to the basic-training camp. After I had passed all the tests, I heard that it was possible to volunteer for a number of specialized units like air-crew school, paratroopers and submarine duty, so I applied for the pilot school as somehow that appealed to me the most. I was sent to a special air-force camp to undergo rigorous tests, both physical and mental. The eye tests alone took close to three hours, but the most difficult evaluations were the theoretical ones. As I had only six and a half years of schooling under my belt and had never been to high school, I didn't place too much hope in passing those.

Until the tests were processed I was sent back to a basic-training camp in Sarafand. This was an old British camp and the discipline of new recruits there was quite brutal, in typical army style. Many of the staff sergeants and sergeants had served in the British forces. To new recruits, they were feared God-like individuals who controlled every minute of our lives. Even seeing them from afar, we became afraid that, God forbid, they might find something wrong with the way we dressed or moved or exercised. I was about two and a half weeks into this torturous regime when a miracle happened. A courier came to the training field where we got our asses burned. The courier was carrying a sealed envelope. After my sergeant opened it, he approached me and showed me the message, indicating that I had to leave the unit and report to the camp where the air-force pilot courses were held. His whole demeanour had changed. The sergeant's tone was surprisingly human as he explained what I had to do. He even shook my hand and wished me good luck!

The harsh behaviour and sometimes brutal demands of our trainers served an important, though often misunderstood, goal. They took all kinds of kids, some quite spoiled, and made them capable of fighting or filling any other posts in the IDF, Israel Defense Forces. From soft rookies, they became responsible soldiers, able to follow orders and work together as a unit to fulfill most jobs they were given to perform. God bless those rough, tough, and many times hated, sergeants. In the training camps, each individual was watched and graded by the trainers to gauge which positions they would perform best in.

When I arrived at the Kfar Sirkin pilot-training camp, course Number 7 had already started and there was no way I could join in. So I had to wait for course Number 8. Until then, I was assigned to work as a military policeman, guarding the main gate of the camp. The camp was not very big, but it was connected to an airfield where all the planes were stationed. Being a military policeman was not bad, as we were on duty twenty-four hours and then free for three days. We were not at the gate twenty-four hours but in the unit's building beside the gate. It contained sleeping quarters, a small dining room and a recreation room. The only thing that bothered me was that course Number 7 was short and comprised only thirty-eight students. Course Number 8, on the other hand, was going to be almost double in size as most of those enrolled would have just graduated from high school. This concerned me, given how much school I had missed.

The pilot course at that time was divided into three sections. First, there was the totally theoretical preparatory section called *machin*, which took three months. If you passed this, you proceeded to the practical part of the flying section, *matchil* in Hebrew. This took place using World War II double-winged Stearman aircraft. This plane was very acrobatic and quite simple to handle with a basic level of knowledge, and students would first fly it with the instructor and later solo. Graduates of the second section moved on to the so-called "progressive" part of the course, which used North American Harvard planes. The lucky ones who finished the course were granted their pilot's wings or, alternatively, they became navigators.

Camp life was quite pleasant; the officers and sergeants behaved rather decently. They demanded the necessary discipline but not to the extreme. Students were evaluated almost daily by the instructors in order to determine who would be better as a pilot and who as a navigator. For course Number 8, we had over 650 candidates. Out of this group, only sixty-two — including me — passed the entry tests. After the course started, we found out that thirty-four at most would be admitted to flying school because of the limited number of aircraft available. Because of this numbers' game, the passing grade for each subject was raised from 51 per cent to 61 per cent.

We had twelve subjects to study. Some were based on high mathematics, like bombing metrology and trigonometry. The tests for each subject were based on a ballot system, which assigned points for each right answer according to the number of questions on the test. For example, let's assume a particular test had thirty-three questions. In that case, each correct answer would be worth three points, plus one, to make up the total of 100 per cent. On the other hand, each mistake deducted six points from the total, so that if the student had seven wrong answers, he flunked the test. The idea behind this double-negative point system was that if the student was not completely sure, he shouldn't answer the question. This relates to the idea that a pilot should not perform any action or manoeuvre if he or she is not 100 per cent confident about it.

These preparatory three months were difficult for me and for many of the other candidates. After the three months had passed and the tests were over, we got our first off-duty weekend. When we came back, everyone ran to the bulletin board where the results were posted. When I saw mine, I felt the biggest disappointment of my life — I had failed. It didn't lessen the pain that another thirty-one candidates, all of them high school graduates, had failed as well. My average on all the twelve subjects was higher than the class average, but I had flunked three subjects, which was more than was accepted in this exceptionally competitive course. I should note that of the 650 candidates from the entering class, only five pilots and two navigators graduated. In retrospect, I should have been proud that I was even allowed to attempt this goal, given my lack of education. Still, my dream of becoming a pilot in the famous Israeli Air Force was gone, and with it the automatic rank of lieutenant.

After these results, six of us received orders to go to another air-force camp for a special course. Despite our failure, we were still part of the Israeli Air Force. When we arrived there, we were told that were going to be trained to be part of a special unit and school called the "air spotters." Before starting the course, we got a few days off. This was greatly welcome, as we had had only the one off-duty weekend in the previous three months.

I went to visit my sister, my cousin in Petah Tikva and Olga and Laci. Then I went to the special dormitory for nursing students. A distinguished older lady was the house mother and she kept a strict code for all visitors except for a few, including me. I was an accepted guest, as three girls from my *mossad* lived there. Even when Kati or one of my other friends was in class, I could go to her room to wait for her. When I told Kati about the great tragedy that had befallen me at the pilot course, instead of feeling sorry for me, she was jumping and hugging me and telling me that she had been praying for that to happen, because she had been very worried about me becoming a pilot. It was true that many graduates of that school didn't have very long lives because of the equipment being used in the early fifties. Also, accidents happened when pilots became cocky and didn't follow the rules and regulations and went too low or flew upside down or in low altitudes. Still, the careful and well-disciplined ones did well. Which was why, at the time, I was really upset that Kati was expressing her happiness about my failure.

After this visit, I went back to the new camp, Tel Nof, to begin the course for air spotters. This took about six weeks of intensive learning. Our officer was Captain Yehuda Ekstein, a pleasant but serious guy. Sergeant Major Cory was his assistant and later, after passing the sergeant's course, I myself became first sergeant when Cory left. The five other guys from the pilot course also became sergeants. Tel Nof was a monster-sized old British camp in southern Israel. It had a very large airfield where fighter squadrons, paratrooper transports and jump planes were stationed. It included all kinds of special school units and two major camps. Our air-spotter school took up six or seven sheet-metal barracks. On the same road to the left of us was the main gate to the paratroopers' training camp and on the right, the main gate to the girls' training camp. Opposite our air-spotter school was a large field used only by the paratroopers for crawling under barbed wire and many other obstacles.

After we all finished the course to become trainers, we started to prepare for our first intake of students. The course ran for two weeks and was intended for reservists, meaning not only youth who had already finished their army duties but anyone who was unable to belong to a fighting unit because of age or some other limiting factor. In Israel, all women, whether single or married, belonged to the reservist units until they had their first child. At that point, they were released from military services. But all men could be in the reserves, so some there were grandfathers. The age range was from twenty-one to fifty-four. There were six of us instructors, ourselves only twenty years old. Anyone in a classroom can become like a child and do things to embarrass their teachers and catch them making mistakes, so we had to handle ourselves well. To teach such a variety of ages and occupations — everybody from street cleaners to professors, writers and tradesmen — and people of different social status gave us the best possible preparation for later life. We learned how to deal with many different kinds of individuals.

The course was intended to teach people to identify all the traffic in Israeli skies. It was not a simple task, as in those days there were a huge number of planes in the air — not only our own and those of our enemies, but also British, French, German, American, Italian and Soviet aircraft. We taught our students to recognize planes from three distinctive views: from the front, when the plane comes toward the spotter; from the bottom, when it passes over the spotter's station; and from the side. The form of each plane is as distinctive as a fingerprint. To help the students recognize them, we projected slides and they had to learn to draw the images they saw on paper. At the outset, we had a great variety of drawings of birds, but slowly they got the hang of it and the birds evolved into recognizable planes.

Eventually, we changed the slides faster and faster to help them identify four types of information: direction, plane type, number of planes and rough estimate of height or altitude. This information was to be sent to the main war room by radio. The war room also constantly received radar information, but radar was sometimes inadequate to catch low-flying aircraft. Combining information from these two sources, the officers in the war room would be able to issue orders to artillery, air force and other units. The country was divided into triangles by air-spotting stations placed on water towers and other high structures. Each station could see into the airspace of other nearby stations, thereby covering the whole country. Each station had its own communication equipment and code by which the four identifying pieces of information were to be transferred to the war room.

For the last morning of each course, we got a light plane resembling a Piper Cub to fly all over at different heights so our students could actually work from life and transfer the necessary information to our war room. On each flight, one of the trainers went up with the pilot. Then after marking the final test and before going home, we arranged to have a celebration with the students. Many of the participants as well as the trainers became friends; some friendships lasted longer than the time six of us lived together in one room. Some even lasted a lifetime.

One such friendship developed with a guy that I first met on the pilot course. From the outset, I became very close to this fellow who had been born in Germany but was less than a year old when his parents moved to Israel. For all intents and purposes, he was a sabra, a born Israeli, and his sense of humour and sharp mind appealed greatly to me. In addition, the resemblance between the two of us was uncanny. His name was Zvi Ben Shabeti, although we called him "Snuci." My Hebrew name is Zvi Benyovits, so there was that similarity between our names, but this was not the end of it. When we dressed in uniform, we looked like twins. We were the same height, the same build and had almost the same smile. Most of the time, we had the same rank. We became very close and this friendship continues even today, in our senior years. I feel privileged that I have been able to maintain my closeness with him, as with all the other important people in my life.

~

Life at Tel Nof was quite enjoyable. The camp was like a large city. It had an excellent swimming pool, a movie theatre, different recreation clubs for different ranks. It was not hard to meet girls from the airforce bases or from the girls' training camp. On days off at the beginning of coming to Tel Nof, I still went to Haifa to visit Kati, who now went by the Hebrew name of Miriam. But then I started to meet other women. One of the course participants was very attractive and interesting, a writer for newspapers and other publications. We somehow hit it off despite our age difference.

Then I met a sergeant from the girls' training camp. Her name was also Miriam. She was a quiet, pleasant individual and a member of a Hashomer Hatzair kibbutz called Ein Shemer. We started to go out together with ever-increasing frequency. Miriam went home to her kibbutz on weekends. Like me, she had almost no family, so the kibbutz was like a family to her. After a while, she invited me to go with her to her kibbutz, where she had her own room. My weekend appearances there quickly became expected, and no one questioned them. I liked the close-knit structure of the kibbutz, but over time, I found many things that I didn't agree with. Maybe I was more of an individualist and just couldn't fit into a structure where everyone was equal and everything was shared. And I soon realized that some people were more equal than others. Meanwhile, Miriam joined my get-togethers with my buddies from the air-spotter school. Snuci was dating a girl from Tel Aviv called Eva. Their relations also got more intimate and we spent a lot of time together as a foursome.

Miriam and I started to plan our future together. We planned to get married when I finished my army duties. In the meantime, my school was transferred to the vicinity of Haifa in the north of Israel, while she was transferred to Sarafand in the middle of the country. This meant total separation, at least during the week. We were both approached by our direct officers to sign up for permanent army careers, which came with a decent income as well as job security. We discussed this but decided against it, worried that our separation would now extend to the weekends as our ranks would require certain duties to be performed then as well. We loved each other and wanted to be together the way other couples were. Although financially the army offer was enticing, we put limits on what we were ready to accept.

During one of my last visits with Kati, I told her about this development and that I wanted us to continue as good friends. Kati was not too happy, but finally she accepted the offered friendship. This friendship, like the one with my buddy Snuci, still continues today after my marriage to Miriam and after Kati's marriage to her husband, Andris, and the kids that followed in both our families.

When Miriam notified the kibbutz of her intention to leave, she and I were treated like lepers, or at least traitors. The kibbutz usually arranged festive weddings for its members but we knew we wouldn't be getting one, so we asked a group of Miriam's friends to organize a trip to a small town nearby where the rabbi lived, who agreed to officiate at our wedding. One of our friends organized a tractor with a platform on which eight guys and Miriam would ride to the rabbi. The rabbi and his son would make up the minyan of ten men over thirteen years of age required for any official religious gathering. To celebrate the event, we took a honey loaf and one bottle of red wine from the military canteen. The ceremony was performed on October 12, 1953. The document registration occurred in another town on October 13, 1953. Our children, Amit and Ronit, still argue about when to celebrate our wedding anniversary, the discrepancy between the two dates giving a pretext for extra fun.

I was released from duty immediately upon getting married. Miriam had another few weeks to go, but her superior officer gave her the time off as a holiday. We started to look for a place to live straightaway, so that we would begin married life with a home base. Simultaneously, a friend of mine from Hungary and the *mossad* let us know that there was a potential job for Miriam at the children's institute in Kiryat Bialik where he worked as an assistant teacher. After an interview, Miriam got the job as supervisor in the institute kitchen, mainly in its dining room. It was not a high-paying job, but it included room and board for both of us. Our living quarters comprised a *tzrif*, a one-room wooden shack, in the middle of the institute's yard. It held a narrow bed, a wooden cabinet and a small table with two chairs. The only window was the small one on the door. All our hygiene services were in another building, but we nonetheless felt lucky and happy to have found such an all-around solution.

Through a distant relative, I got a job in a granite-polishing shop. I worked with water all day in special rubber boots, wearing a rubber apron. It was an awful job, but luckily, I didn't need it for too long. After my release from the army, I found out that a defence ministry factory close to Haifa was looking for tradesmen, including lathe operators. This was the job I had apprenticed for in Hungary. After I went to the factory and filled out an application, I was told it would take some time for the security check to be completed, but that I would be notified if I got the job. It took a few nervous weeks, but I finally got my acceptance in the mail. I worked in a room where we prepared tools for many different automated production machines. Great precision was required since each production machine had a set of instruments to test every part before it progressed to the next section. It was a dream job for me as this factory, despite its large workforce, was fully unionized with good wages and excellent social benefits. The factory even had its own kitchen and dining room, where first-rate meals were supplied at no cost to us.

The factory was quite far from Kiryat Bialik, but it provided transportation since many workers lived in that area. On the truck trips to and from the factory, I met my dearest friend, Rami Vardy. An ex-paratrooper and a genius at most things he touched, he worked for the testing department where he progressed rapidly to become the assistant manager. This testing department had more authority than the general manager of the factory. If they didn't pass a product, then the product was rejected or had to be reworked. Rami's position involved a lot of travelling to meetings and seminars both within Israel and abroad. He and his wife, Rochelle, became our best friends and we spent a lot of time together. Because they were both Israeli-born, they had lots of friends roughly the same age as us from school or from Zionist groups, and we became part of this group; ultimately, we were eight couples. Later, we all had children at around the same time.

In the meantime, we moved from our shack to better and better accommodations, until we were finally able to acquire a beautiful apartment by paying *schlissel gelt*, key money. We were on the street level with a big balcony and a garden. Our ceilings were five metres (or over fifteen feet) high as was customary, because the added height drew the heat up in the summer, keeping the living areas cooler. The custom of our group dictated that we take turns hosting each other on Friday evenings. We had the most spacious place for card games or sing-alongs; the other seven couples always teased us good-naturedly, because they were all sabras and yet lived in the small government-subsidized apartments while we, the *olim*, lived in relative luxury. This didn't make our participation in the group any less enjoyable.

We toured the country with these friends as well as going on factory-arranged trips for employees at holiday times. This is how we first visited Eilat, a town on the Red Sea in the southernmost section of Israel. We slept outdoors under the sky, which was hot but very romantic, because Eilat was in the desert and not developed in those days. Now, it is a world-famous tropical resort with super-modern hotels where tourists go to scuba dive among beautiful coral reefs. We also took trips to Masada, a historical site where Jewish zealots committed suicide rather than be taken into slavery by the Romans; Masada has come to symbolize the motto "never again." The stables of the Roman camp can clearly be seen below the ruins of the Jewish dwellings. One can also see the huge ramp built by the Romans for their catapults and other materials used in the attack. Many IDF units have their graduating ceremonies up on Masada in the ruins of King Herod's castle, usually early in the morning when the sun starts to rise above the horizon. This is also a favourite place to hold bar mitzvahs. The view of the Judean deserts and mountains from the top is indescribably majestic.

It didn't matter to us that these trips were made on trucks with nothing but hard benches to sit on. We weren't spoiled since we had just left the army. Besides, to keep in shape as reservists, we had to put in yearly training periods, the length of which depended on one's rank but usually were at least ten days long. Quite often in those days, emergencies were declared because of acts of terrorism or other special situations. In such cases, you were called to duty by special codes broadcast over the radio or, if you happened to be already on reserve duty, your tour was extended if necessary.

Besides the customary Friday night get-togethers, our group also went to the seashore on Saturday mornings. All of us lived in the *krayot*, suburbs, of Kiryat Haim, Kiryat Motzkin and Kiryat Bialik spread along the road from Haifa to Acre. Each *kiryah* was bicycle distance from the sea. Sometimes in convoy, other times singly, we pedalled to our special meeting place by the sea. We stayed until midday, and then we went home from the scorching noon sunshine to rest. In the late afternoon, we met again to go to the movies. Our social life around our group was quite intense. If that was not enough, sometimes mid-week after dinner we took our bikes out for a ride. As so many people in our area knew us, soon after starting to pedal we would stop for a short chat. This same scenario was repeated again and again as we cycled over to our friends' houses. It didn't matter what they were doing when we arrived; we always felt welcome.

But our relationship with Rami and Rochelle was something even more special than our friendship with the group. We four were inseparable. We became part of their family and vice versa, although Miriam and I had very little to offer by way of family gatherings. We often went to visit Rami's parents, who lived close to us. Both his parents were exceptionally warm and enjoyable to visit. They had a detached house, which included a good-sized garden with all kinds of fruit trees and a vegetable plot; this was a big plus in the early years after our army service, when Israel suffered from the lack of many basics like fruit, among other commodities.

It was rare that we had the chance to get together and talk with our best buddies from the army, Snuci and Eva. They lived in Tel Aviv, while we were in the *kiryot* far north of them, which made communication difficult between us. We had neither telephones nor cars; communication depended on a few words in a letter and the occasional meeting during a holiday. But even now, all these years later, whenever we get together we feel as if we haven't been parted for a single day. The closeness between the four of us hasn't suffered one iota. I feel that this is a special gift in one's life that has to be cherished, as many people never get to experience such close friendship. We feel the same way about Rami and Rochelle and so have experienced a double blessing.

An Emotional Farewell

In early 1959 most of the girls in our group became pregnant, although I don't remember a general meeting declaring it was time to bring a new generation into being. Perhaps the girls decided this among themselves! Our son, Amit, joined us on August 29, 1959. Amit means "friend" in Hebrew. He was also given the names of two of his deceased grandfathers: Joel (Miriam's father) and David (my late father). It is a Jewish tradition for a newborn to carry on the memory of a departed relative, so his given name is Amit Joel David.

He was born on a Saturday, and Miriam worked until the last minute on Friday. First, she bicycled home from work at the *mossad* in Kiryat Bialik and then, as if that wasn't enough effort, she got down on her knees to do some serious cleaning. Before Amit's arrival, we had negotiated with the apartment's owner to add a separate room for the expected newcomer. This required breaking through a wall to create a connecting door. Somehow, we planned this work too close to Amit's arrival. The work was finished, but there was a lot of cleaning left to do. Miriam resolved to do a perfect job but it was too much for her, so she accepted my help. This desire to do things perfectly has continued throughout our lives together, God bless her. Toward the end of the day, she started to feel cramps and pain and we rushed to the hospital with the best obstetrics department, which was on Mount Carmel. A few hours later, our beautiful, healthy son arrived. It was one of the happiest and proudest times of our lives.

Eight days later, most of our friends and acquaintances attended the precious event of our son's *brit*, circumcision ceremony. My only regret and sorrow was that none of our parents could share this milestone and derive *naches*, pleasure, from their first grandchild. My mother, who had moved briefly to Israel in the early 1950s to live with my sister Magda in Ramat HaSharon, was now living in Canada with my sister Edith. Miriam's mother would make aliyah eventually but hadn't arrived yet.

Amit grew at a fast pace and before he was one year old, he could already run around and speak several words. Close behind was Rami and Rochelle's son Eyal, a lively little devil who brought a lot of pleasure to all of us. Now all the bicycles had little chairs on their front bars. Sometimes, all three of us travelled on one bicycle, with Miriam sitting on the package rack, Amit on the front and me in the middle.

I felt as though I had come a long way. I went through the hell of hells during World War II. I survived, but I lost most of my family. I also lost my education and my innocence. It took two major attempts, but I had finally succeeded in leaving Hungary and fulfilling my dream to come to Israel, where I tried to make a contribution to my beloved country through my military service. In the army, I found a friend, lover and wife with whom to go through life. I should have been content but as often happens, the devil started to work on me and I ended up doing something I never thought I would.

I already noted that I was not cut out for kibbutz life because I was an individualist. I wanted to prove to myself and to the world that I could provide a decent future for my family by creating my own business. Because I worked in the Israeli defence industry as a lathe operator, my dream was to set up my own machine shop in Israel. But given the income I had at that time, such a dream was almost unachievable. While I was thinking about such things, Martha, a third cousin from Canada, came to visit some of her relatives who lived on a kibbutz and also paid a visit to us.

After the Hungarian Revolution occurred in 1956, Joe, the husband of my first cousin Edit Weltman, flew over to Vienna where he hired several smugglers and gave each a few names and addresses of people to bring out of Hungary. Because of Joe's incredible actions, all of my mother's brothers with their new wives as well as her first, second and third cousins — some twelve families altogether — made it out. They all settled in Toronto. Eventually, most of them worked in a hosiery factory that belonged to a friend of one of my uncles. He was the first to start to work in this place, but slowly he brought in some six or seven relatives of ours.

All my relatives had been extremely religious, and most had lost their children in the Holocaust. Now, they didn't have great financial demands for things like TV, radios or travelling, so I think they were content to work at low-paying jobs. Their only expenses were accommodation, food, clothing and synagogue dues. They all lived around Bathurst and College, on Palmerston, Markham and Euclid, which was then the Hungarian-Jewish neighbourhood. Their apartments were quite inexpensive and they had succeeded in accumulating savings. So when Martha came to Israel and we asked her what she thought about us going to Canada to save up the approximately $10,000 US we required to equip a machine shop, she gave us a very rosy assessment. She said that being a tradesman, I would do well there and that Miriam would be able to pay a babysitter for Amit about eight or nine dollars a week so that she could work and we could also save her income.

Being cautious, we halved her calculations; even so, it seemed that we would be able to achieve our goals in only two to three years. In 1962, to make such a drastic move involved a lot of preparation. Miriam's employers felt sorry to lose her, but our biggest problem was notifying my work about our pending departure. The management took it quite hard. During my roughly nine years with the defence ministry's factory, I had become something of a leader among the workers. We had a lot of grievances about how the Histadrut, our union, forced all kinds of financial arrangements upon us workers, which were against our interest. I started a fight for a better arrangement, and I was respected by the general management as well as by the union big shots. They didn't like my rebellious ideas, but they understood that I could get the cooperation of the majority of the workforce. This was not simple to achieve in our workplace, where most workers were card-carrying members of the Labour party and the Histadrut. At any rate, when I notified the management of my intention to move to Canada, I suddenly became a traitor. That reaction was almost universal in those days: Anyone who left Israel was seen to be running away from the difficulties and dangers the country faced. It didn't matter that we claimed that our absence would be short. They all assumed that, as usual, it would turn into a permanent departure. In hindsight, they were right and we were wrong.

The Canadian visa requirements were that someone had to sponsor us so that, in case of need, we wouldn't become a burden to the authorities. We started selling all our belongings once we had an indication from the Canadian consulate that things were progressing well. Then, without warning, our visa application was denied. This came upon us like a lightning bolt. We no longer had jobs, an apartment, furnishings, nothing. We ran frantically back and forth to the consulate for two to three weeks until they discovered a mistake in our application. Although I had stopped smoking when I left the army, I started again. It was one of the most stressful times we'd experienced up until then, although later on we had a few worse episodes in our business life.

Slowly, we made all the necessary arrangements. We bought tickets for the boat to New York and the flight from New York to Toronto. We started to say our painful goodbyes — to my sister Magda and to all our other relatives and especially to our friends. For me, the hardest separations were from my army buddy Snuci Ben Shabeti and his wife, Eva, and from my best buddy from work, Rami Vardi, and his wife, Rochelle. Also, Miriam's mother had arrived from Romania just three years before we decided to make our move to Canada, so it was doubly hard for her that after so many years of not having her daughter with her, they had to part again. The only consolation was that she'd found a wonderful man named Lazar, and with him at her side, she wouldn't feel so lonely. They married just before our departure.

The whole gang of friends and all our relatives came to the port of Haifa in late May 1962 to see us off. It was an emotional farewell full of promises from both sides to keep in touch as much as possible.

The ship we sailed on, the SS *United States*, was a good-sized 45,000-ton passenger ship with all the modern facilities. The ship arrived in New York and after disembarking, we went to the immigration station with our papers and were notified that we needed an escort to accompany us from the boat terminal to the airport for our flight to Toronto. We went in a taxi and a police escort stayed with us until we boarded our flight. This treatment made us feel like we were criminals. It was an unpleasant welcome to North America.

On our arrival in Toronto, my mother and sister were waiting to welcome us. Meeting Edith for the first time since 1949 was especially emotional. Of course, seeing beautiful almost three-year-old Amit for the first time, Mother couldn't get enough of him. Even though Amit and his grandmother Helen and his aunt Edith didn't speak the same language, they somehow understood each other.

Edith lived on a dairy farm about an hour from Toronto with her husband, Martin, and my mother had joined them there. We all drove back together in Edith's car. For us, the novelty of life on the farm was fun for a short time. Amit especially enjoyed the dog, the tractor and the pickup my sister used when she went to Toronto once a week to do her food shopping and other errands. But we soon became aware of how hard their lives were. They had arrived after the Hungarian Revolution, and since their arrival they had never managed to leave the farm for even one night. They didn't even have a radio, so the first thing we did was buy them one. We were overwhelmed by disappointment to see such a lifestyle in 1962 in Canada. This was especially hard for my sister, who had grown up comfortably in Budapest.

At the same time that Edith and Martin had arrived in Canada, our other uncles and aunts came, too. All of them settled in Toronto and worked at simple jobs that provided a decent living. My stubborn brother-in-law was the only one who declared that he didn't want to be anybody else's slave. When he found out that some Baron de Hirsch farms were available for Jewish newcomers, he jumped at the offer. He didn't become a slave of anyone but the cows and the feed and milk companies that sucked so much out of them that they didn't have a chance to save, but instead went deeper and deeper into debt. In Israel, someone who had three to four cows was able to make a living. But on their farm with more than eighty cows, they couldn't attain the minimum services the poorest city-dweller had. The farm was a good size but the house they lived in was a disaster — no running water, no heating, no bath or toilet except an outhouse. At least a shower was available at the modern milk storage and cooling building, which was a part of the conditions the milk company demanded before signing a contract.

The dairy farming also didn't provide enough income for them to hire help or buy a few things that would have made their lives more bearable. And to go out in the summer, and especially in the winter in knee-high snow at 4:00 a.m. to start milking and spend the rest of the day working in the barn and the fields was surely worse than the "slavery" suffered by our relatives in the city. It was heartbreaking to see my beautiful sister in these conditions.

My cousin's husband, Joe, who had brought all our families to Canada after the Hungarian Revolution, arranged for me to work at a friend's machine shop. But I couldn't start work until we found accommodation in the city. Joe wanted us to live in the same area as our relatives, but when we looked at available places in that neighbourhood, Miriam got really upset, as she couldn't see how Amit could live without any green areas to play on. I agreed with her; after leaving such a beautiful apartment in Israel, I couldn't see us living in those conditions, either. After all, we didn't come to Canada as refugees, fleeing unbearable conditions. We came to fulfill a dream but were not willing to sacrifice our lifestyle for it. This was not snobbery, just the facts.

At any rate, we met an Israeli friend who suggested we consider the area where many Israelis lived in buildings of six apartments each. It was not luxurious, since the buildings were quite old, but the facilities had been updated. The most favourable point for us was that it provided a large green space for kids to play in. Also, it was right beside the Associated Hebrew School that had classes from junior kindergarten up. Another thing that got our attention was the Baycrest Hospital and old-age complex, a place of possible employment for Miriam.

We leased a two-bedroom apartment with a living room, a kitchen and a good-sized balcony on Wasdale Crescent near Bathurst and Wilson. It was not cheap, but we felt that this was what we needed to have a decent life. Edith took us to a furniture store where we bought the bare minimum. We lived on the second floor, one long block from Bathurst Street, which provided public transportation. We later learned that Bathurst was the main hub for the Jews of Toronto.

We arrived in Canada with a little more than $2,000, which was all we had left after the sale of our apartment and other belongings, and after the cost of travel to Canada. In 1962, it would seem to be a reasonable sum, but it was actually insufficient to cover the cost of starting over in Toronto. Instead of eating up the little reserve we had, it was urgent for us to find jobs — any jobs — that would bring in some income. So I went with Joe to his friend Max's shop. As soon as I saw him, I realized we had gone to the same Orthodox school in Budapest before the deportations. The lathe available for me to do my work was in terrible shape. Instead of drilling into cast iron rods itself, it had to be pushed by sheer force. I was used to working diligently at my job in Israel, but this was an unheard-of method of work and made the job hard and frustrating.

Then came the pay. Max paid me $1.65 per hour or about $66.00

per week gross. After deductions, I received less than $55.00, and from this I had to pay for my transportation and food. It took two weeks of pay to cover the cost of renting our apartment. Clearly, the calculations made by Martha, our Canadian visitor to Israel, had been out of whack. My income didn't even cover our basic expenses. So after a few weeks working for Max, I started to look for a better-paying job.

The metal fabrication industry was quite busy with the Korean War going on; the newspaper listings were full of jobs for tradesmen, including lathe operators. So, with the paper in hand, I started hunting. Each sizable company had a questionnaire for the applicants. Along with all the regular questions, one asked where the applicant came from. As I wasn't in the habit of hiding my nationality, I faithfully wrote "Israel." And in every place, I got the same reaction — *We are sorry but the position was already filled.* I was rejected by twelve companies in all. The interesting thing was that all the companies that I approached continued to advertise their need for my skills.

I am not a quitter. The thirteenth company I visited was in the vicinity of Pape and Danforth Avenue. The company's name was Extrusion Machinery Company. They produced dies for the extrusion of plastic products. This company had no form to fill out. The foreman, Paul, gave me a drawing and a piece of material and showed me to a vacant lathe. He simply said that he would decide whether or not he would hire me after I had finished the job. If I were successful, he would then tell me the hourly rate for starting work. I finished the job and Paul said he would hire me with a starting salary of $2.15. This was fifty cents more than Max gave me and, more importantly, it was a well-equipped shop with over 120 employees.

The only problem that I had to solve was the distance of my place of employment from where I lived. Eventually, after trying to commute and arrange for lifts to public transportation, we bought a used car, a basic 1957 Ford with no air conditioning. We paid $600 for it. When my cousin Joe saw it he almost flipped; he constantly tried to convince us that we couldn't afford it. He rejected the idea that it was a necessity for me to get to work, especially given the upcoming winter weather. Given that he and many of his peers came to Canada straight from the camps, they were happy with the simple accommodations. We, on the other hand, had given up a beautiful apartment in Israel and our new one was inferior to what we were used to. So buying a car improved our quality of life and allowed us to do many more things. We wanted to see our friends and our relatives and take holidays when work allowed them.

Meanwhile, Miriam enrolled in a bookkeeping course. This served a double purpose: bookkeeping as a future employment opportunity and the opportunity to learn English. Her first job was way downtown, so she had to leave early in the morning to get there in time and we had to find a babysitter for Amit. Her pay cheque was so meagre that after paying the babysitter and her travelling costs, she had only five to ten dollars left over for the week, a week during which she spent eleven hours a day out of the house.

Soon, she left this job to work in the office of the same factory where our relatives worked. She didn't divulge that her relations were working there. This job provided shorter days and a bit better pay. Luckily, she had also applied to Baycrest Hospital for a bookkeeping job, even before her evening course was complete. It took a long time to get a positive reply but when she did, it was worth it. She assisted the purchasing manager of pharmaceuticals, a Hungarian woman named Mrs. Goldberg. This manager became Miriam's good friend, especially when her son and Amit started to go to kindergarten together at the Hebrew school.

Realizing that our current earning capabilities would provide little chance to fulfill the dream of accumulating enough money to go back and open a machine shop in Israel, I started to look in other directions. First, I realized that the lathes and milling machines provided by the Extrusion Machinery Company were inferior for working on hard materials than comparable Iscar machines I had used in Israel. So I contacted the company to see if they would be interested in my representing them in Canada, and possibly all over North America. They answered in the positive. I visited a number of good-sized machine shops, explaining that I could provide them with carbide tools substantially better than what they were using at a lower price than they were paying. Of course, they all showed interest and provided me with lists of the cutter shapes and sizes of the pieces they used monthly. I promised them samples to try. Paul, the foreman of the company where I worked, gave me the same information and I told him that I would bring in a small shipment of test pieces free for trial if he promised he would order some if he liked them. The answer was yes.

On the basis of all the positive responses I got, I put together an order, part of which would be given free to all the companies to try and the other part of which would be sold to Paul for the Extrusion Machinery Company. I borrowed $5,000.00 to pay for this order. According to the prices given to me by Iscar and the existing prices of the present suppliers, even if I provided better cutters for about 30 per cent less than the local ones, I would still make good money.

On the surface, my idea looked fine, but one factor I didn't take into account was that the companies wouldn't give up the security of their present suppliers without being sure that I would be able to service them on a timely basis. They would all try the Iscar products on a small scale, but to switch over entirely to foreign products was another matter. For example, after trying my cutters, Paul found them way better than those he had used for many years. Nonetheless, he placed a very small order from me, one that did not cover all his needs. My second mistake was that I didn't realize how much capital would be needed to accumulate sufficient inventory for the varied needs of just a few companies. The acquisition of all the many different shapes and sizes of cutters used on lathes and milling machines was out of my league. I needed to line up a wealthy partner to succeed, but I didn't have one.

Just to demonstrate the validity of my idea, 80 per cent of Iscar was sold to the famous businessman Warren Buffett for four billion US dollars in 2006; the remaining 20 per cent was sold to his company in 2013. Representing Iscar in North America would have produced enormous wealth for me, even back in my days. Iscar became the sole supplier of all the carbide tools Black & Decker sold and many of the largest industries started to use Iscar cutters.

I needed to learn a lot to succeed in business in North America. It was becoming increasingly clear that my dream of returning to our lives in the land of my Zionist dreams was becoming more and more unattainable. First, all the calculations we had relied on were totally different from the reality; our original goal of accumulating $10,000 US in capital was inadequate. Second, this goal constantly increased at a faster rate than our earnings did. The dream that had started back when I was an eight-year-old in Budapest in 1940 lasted only until 1962 in Toronto, when my misguided quest to become an independent machine-shop owner in Israel was blown away like a light cloud that no amount of hope would bring back.

Epilogue

In the end, I did succeed in owning an independent shop — Auto V Grooving Inc. — and over the forty years I was in business, I produced some clever machinery that made a lot of our customers wealthy, but the frustration and the constant tension our business created was a stiff price to pay. However, our family happily grew — our daughter, Ronit, was born in Canada in 1968 — and we were able to provide our children with excellent educations and a good basis for their futures. Our kids brought us a lot of happiness, especially later in our lives with the arrival of our grandchildren — Amit's Jamie and Ronit's Josh and Rebecca — which made our lives a lot more bearable. I still hope to be able to spend some time in the land of my dreams but that looks unlikely, as Miriam can't see herself away from our children and especially our grandchildren, even for a month or two. I follow every event that happens in Israel and keep hoping that one day Israelis will achieve a liveable agreement with their Arab neighbours.

When I was in Israel in the late 1970s — after fifteen years, I finally succeeded in getting back there — I visited the youth institution that I was at when I arrived in Israel, Kibbutz Tel Yitzhak. I was talking to the director, who welcomed me with open arms, about the fact that I felt that documentation about the Zionist organizations in Budapest was not done, and that proper recognition was not given. He told me that I was quite in luck, because the kibbutz had established a museum and institute for teaching the Holocaust called the Massuah. At the time, the museum concentrated on the youth of that period, through their personal letters, postcards and so on.

When the kids came there to learn, they were led into a hall where there were six stones symbolizing the six million people that died in the Holocaust. On the subject of resistance, it is necessary to safeguard, in the right light and position, what resistance activities required during that period of wartime. In Budapest, there were absolutely amazing, brave actions that youngsters — kids of sixteen, seventeen — carried out. In every second of their activities, they endangered their lives. They could have avoided this danger and in my book, this is real heroism. The generation of witnesses older than me are gone, so I have told my life story mainly to put into words the heroic activities of the youngsters working in the Hungarian Zionist underground during the war years. According to my knowledge, little else has been written about their actions, actions that contributed to saving untold numbers of our desperate brethren in their darkest hours, Hungarian Jews who were the last remnant of a huge and vibrant Jewish community.

I want the next generations to know about these bright points that we can be proud of, and honour ourselves and our names. We need every point of light that we can find.

Glossary

aliyah (Hebrew; pl. *aliyot*, literally, ascent) A term used by Jews and modern Israelis to refer to Jewish immigration to Israel; the term is also used to refer to "going up" to the altar in a synagogue to read from the Torah.

Aliyah Bet (Hebrew) A clandestine movement established to bring Jewish immigrants without immigration permits to British Mandate Palestine before, during and after World War II. The name, which means "ascent B," differentiates the movement from the immigrants to whom the British granted permits. Aliyah Bet organized ships to pick up Jewish immigrants from different points on the European coast in order to make the perilous journey to Palestine. Many were turned back. *See also* aliyah.

Aliyat Hano'ar (Youth Aliyah) An organization founded in Germany in 1933 by Recha Freier to save Jewish children from the Nazis by sending them to boarding schools and kibbutzim in Palestine. After World War II, Youth Aliyah brought orphaned Jewish children from displaced persons camps in Europe to youth villages in Israel, where they lived and studied. An estimated 5,000 children were brought to Palestine before World War II and another 15,000 after the war. Youth Aliyah later became a department of the Jewish Agency for Israel. To this day, Youth Aliyah helps vulnerable Jewish children from around the world and at-risk Israeli youth by providing them with a supportive home in a youth village in Israel. *See also* kibbutz.

Allies The coalition of countries that fought against Germany, Italy and Japan (the Axis nations). At the beginning of World War II in September 1939, the coalition included France, Poland and Britain. Once Germany invaded the USSR in June 1941 and the United States entered the war following the bombing of Pearl Harbor by Japan on December 7, 1941, the main leaders of the Allied powers became Britain, the USSR and the United States. Other Allies included Canada, Australia, Czechoslovakia, Greece, Mexico, Brazil, South Africa and China. *See also* Axis.

American Jewish Joint Distribution Committee (JDC) Colloquially known as the Joint, the JDC was a charitable organization founded in 1914 to provide humanitarian assistance and relief to Jews all over the world in times of crisis. It provided material support for persecuted Jews in Germany and other Nazi-occupied territories and facilitated their immigration to neutral countries such as Portugal, Turkey and China. Between 1939 and 1944, Joint officials helped close to 81,000 European Jews find asylum in various parts of the world.

Arrow Cross Party (in Hungarian, Nyilaskeresztes Párt – Hungarista Mozgalom; abbreviation: Nyilas) A Hungarian nationalistic and antisemitic party founded by Ferenc Szálasi in 1935 under the name the Party of National Will. With the full support of Nazi Germany, the newly renamed Arrow Cross Party ran in Hungary's 1939 election and won 25 per cent of the vote. The party was banned shortly after the elections, but was legalized again in March 1944 when Germany occupied Hungary. Under Nazi approval, the party assumed control of Hungary from October 15, 1944, to March 1945, led by Szálasi under the name the Government of National Unity. The Arrow Cross regime was particularly brutal toward Jews – in addition to the thousands of Hungarian Jews who had been deported to Nazi death camps during the previous Miklós Horthy regime, the Arrow Cross, during their short period of rule, instigated the murder of tens of thousands of Hungarian Jews. In one specific incident on November 8, 1944, more than 70,000 Jews were rounded up and sent on a death march to Nazi camps in Austria. Between December 1944 and January 1945, the Arrow Cross murdered approximately 20,000 Jews, many of whom had been forced into a closed ghetto at the end of November 1944.

Axis The coalition of countries that included Germany, Italy and Japan that fought against the Allies during World War II. The Axis powers formally signed an agreement of cooperation, the Tripartite Pact, in September 1940. Other countries that joined the Axis included Hungary, Romania, Slovakia, Bulgaria, Yugoslavia and the Independent State of Croatia. *See also* Allies.

bar mitzvah (Hebrew; literally, one to whom commandments apply) The age of thirteen when, according to Jewish tradition, boys become religiously and morally responsible for their actions and are considered adults for the purpose of synagogue ritual. A bar mitzvah is also the synagogue ceremony and family celebration that mark the attainment of this status, during which the boy is called upon to read a portion of the Torah and recite the prescribed prayers in a public prayer forum. In the latter half of the twentieth century, liberal Jews instituted an equivalent ceremony and celebration for girls called a bat mitzvah.

Baron de Hirsch A fund established by the wealthy German Jewish philanthropist Baron Maurice de Hirsch (1831–1896) to provide resettlement assistance to Jewish immigrants who were facing poverty and persecution in Eastern Europe. Believing that Jews could best support themselves by farming, Hirsch established the Jewish Colonization Association, which set up agricultural settlements for Jewish immigrants in Canada, the United States, Argentina, Brazil and Palestine.

Billitzer, Dajnus (Adonyahu) (1913–2005) (also known by his alias, László Dunka) A high school principal, ordained rabbi and member of the Hungarian Zionist youth resistance organization Hanoar Hatzioni. Dr. Billitzer escaped deportations in Debrecen, Hungary, and fled to Budapest with a small group of young Jews. There they joined the underground and participated in resistance efforts. *See also* Hanoar Hatzioni.

British Mandate Palestine The area of the Middle East under British rule from 1923 to 1948, as established by the League of Nations after World War I. During that time, the United Kingdom severely restricted Jewish immigration. The Mandate area encompassed present-day Israel, Jordan, the West Bank and the Gaza Strip.

Budapest ghetto The area established by the government of Hungary on November 29, 1944. By December 10, the ghetto and its 33,000 Jewish inhabitants were sealed off from the rest of the city. At the end of December, Jews who had previously held "protected" status (many by the Swedish government) were moved into the ghetto, and the number of residents increased to 55,000; by January 1945, the number had reached 70,000. The ghetto was overcrowded and lacked sufficient food, water and sanitation. Supplies dwindled and conditions worsened during the Soviet siege of Budapest and thousands died of starvation and disease. Soviet forces liberated the ghetto on January 18, 1945.

cantor (in Hebrew, *chazzan*) A person who leads a Jewish congregation in prayer. Because music plays such a large role in Jewish religious services, the cantor is usually professionally trained in music.

Columbus camp A prison camp in Budapest at 46 Columbus Street, at the Wechselmann Institute for the Deaf. In June 1944, as a result of negotiations between Nazi leader Adolf Eichmann and Zionist leader Rudolf Kasztner, 388 Jews from the Kolozsvár ghetto were selected to be transferred to this "privileged" camp, which was guarded by SS officers who were told to treat the inmates humanely. The camps' inmates were under the impression that they were en route to Palestine. The camp grew rapidly and soon included an infirmary, workshops, religious services and classes that emphasized preparing for life in Palestine. On June 30, 1944, a group of 1,684 people — including many prominent Jews — boarded "Katszner's train" which took them to Bergen-Belsen, and eventually to Switzerland. After that, the population of the Columbus camp grew to 690 people, some Jews paying enormous amounts of money to get in, hopeful that there would be a second train leaving to Palestine. The emblem of the International Red Cross was hung at the entrance to camp identifying it as a refuge for Jews, but the camp was eventually liquidated, with the older Jews sent to the Pest ghetto and the younger Jews marched toward Germany. *See also* Kasztner, Rudolf.

Communist Party of Hungary First founded in 1918 and resurrected in 1945 following the liberation and occupation of Hungary by the Soviet Union. The Party was assisted both openly and clandestinely by the USSR and initially had the support of many Hungarians who had opposed the wartime pro-Nazi government in Hungary. The Communist Party merged with the Social Democratic Party in 1948 and was renamed the Hungarian Workers' Party; it consolidated total power in Hungary by 1949, which it held until 1989.

displaced persons (DPs) People who find themselves homeless and stateless at the end of a war. Following World War II, millions of people, especially European Jews, found that they had no homes to return to or that it was unsafe to do so. To resolve the staggering refugee crisis that resulted, Allied authorities and the United Nations Relief and Rehabilitation Administration (UNRRA) established Displaced Persons (DP) camps to provide temporary shelter and assistance to refugees, and help them transition towards resettlement.

Eagle's Nest (in German, Kehlsteinhaus) A chalet in the Bavarian Alps commissioned by Nazi officials in 1937 as a birthday gift to Adolf Hitler. The Eagle's Nest was used as a meeting place by the Nazi Party and as a place to entertain important political visitors. The site was used infrequently by Hitler because of his aversion to heights and a fear that lightning would strike the house. The Eagle's Nest is now a popular tourist destination.

forced labour battalions (also Labour Service; in Hungarian, *Munkaszolgálat*) Hungary's military-related labour service system, which was first established in 1919 for those considered too "politically unreliable" for regular military service. After the labour service was made compulsory in 1939, Jewish men of military age were recruited to serve; however, having been deemed "unfit" to bear arms, they were equipped with tools and employed in mining, road and rail construction and maintenance work. Though the men were treated relatively well at first, the system became increasingly punitive in nature. By 1941, Jews in forced labour battalions were required to wear a yellow armband and civilian clothes; they had no formal rank and were unarmed; they were often mistreated by extremely antisemitic supervisors; and their work included clearing minefields, causing their death. Between 20,000 and 40,000 Jewish men died during their forced labour service.

gimnázium (Hungarian; in German, *Gymnasium*) A word used throughout Central and Eastern Europe to mean high school or secondary school.

Glass House A safe house established in Budapest in 1944 by Swiss diplomat Carl Lutz. Lutz declared the building, which had once been a glass factory, an annex of the Swiss legation, and gave refuge to thousands of Jews there. The Glass House was also used as headquarters for the Zionist youth movement who made it a centre for document forging and distribution. More than 2,000 people were in the Glass House when it was liberated on January 18, 1945. *See also* Lutz, Carl.

Hanoar Hatzioni (Hebrew) The Zionist Youth. A socialist-Zionist group that began in Europe in 1926 to educate youth in Jewish and Zionist principles and to encourage self-actualization through living in Israel. *See also* Zionism.

Hatikvah (Hebrew; literally, the hope) A poem composed by Naphtali Herz Imber in 1878 that was set to a folk melody and adopted by early Zionist groups in Europe as their anthem, including the First Zionist Congress in 1897. When the State of Israel was established in 1948, it was unofficially proclaimed the national anthem; it officially became so in 2004.

Histadrut (Hebrew; abbreviation of HaHistadrut HaKlalit shel Ha-Ovdim B'Eretz Yisrael; in English, General Federation of Labourers in the Land of Israel) A labour union established in pre-state Israel in 1920. A branch was established in Montreal in 1943.

Hungarian Revolution (1956) A spontaneous uprising against the Soviet-backed Communist government of Hungary in October 1956, the Hungarian Revolution led to the brief establishment of a reformist government under Prime Minister Imre Nagy. The revolution was swiftly crushed by the Soviet invasion of November 1956, during which thousands of civilians were killed.

Jewish Brigade A battalion that was formed in September 1944 under the command of the British Eighth Army. The Jewish Brigade included more than five thousand volunteers from Palestine. After the war, the Brigade was essential in helping Jewish refugees and organizing their entry into Palestine. It was disbanded by the British in 1946.

Jewish houses (Budapest) Also known as "yellow star" buildings (*sárga csillagos házak*). In June 1944, three months after Germany occupied Hungary, the Nazis ordered the Jews in Budapest to move into designated buildings marked with a yellow Star of David. More than 200,000 Jews were assigned to fewer than two thousand apartments. They were allowed to leave the buildings for two hours in the afternoon, but only if they wore an identifying yellow Star of David on their clothing. This meant they could be easily located when the time came for them to be deported. *See also* Budapest ghetto; Star of David.

Kasztner, Rudolf (also, Kastner, Rezső)(1906–1957) Head of the Budapest Relief and Rescue Committee during World War II and infamous for his part in the "blood for trucks" negotiations with Adolf Eichmann that led to what became known as "Kasztner's train" – the release of 1,684 prominent Hungarian Jews to the neutral country of Switzerland in 1944. After the war, Kasztner's role in the negotiations was highly controversial: some viewed him as a collaborator while others applauded him for saving as many lives as he could under the circumstances. Kasztner was assassinated in Israel in 1957 after a widely publicized libel trial, the purpose of which had been to defend accusations against him but instead turned into a moral, politicized examination of his actions during the war. Although most of the guilty verdict was overturned in 1958, the original judge's oft-quoted ruling, that Kasztner "sold his soul to the devil," is still the subject of much debate.

kibbutz (Hebrew) A collectively owned farm or settlement in Israel, democratically governed by its members.

Komoly, Ottó (also Nathan Ze'ev Kohn) (1882–1945) President of the Hungarian Zionist Association and founder of the Budapest Relief and Rescue Committee with Rudolf Kasztner. Komoly, a prominent leader in the rescue efforts of Hungarian Jews, participated in negotiations with the Nazis and Hungarian officials and supported the resistance activities of Zionist youth groups. In his position as head of "Department A" of the International Red Cross, Komoly set up safe houses for children in Budapest in 1944. It is estimated that the safe houses he set up saved 5,000 to 6,000 children. Komoly was abducted and killed by members of the Arrow Cross on January 1, 1945. *See also* Arrow Cross Party; Kasztner, Rudolf.

kosher (Hebrew) Fit to eat according to Jewish dietary laws. Observant Jews follow a system of rules known as *kashruth* that regulates what can be eaten, how food is prepared and how animals and poultry are slaughtered. Food is kosher when it has been deemed fit for consumption according to this system of rules. There are several foods that are forbidden, most notably pork products and shellfish.

Levente (abbreviation of Levente Egyesületek; Hungarian; literally, knight) A paramilitary youth corps established in Hungary in 1921. Youth between the ages of twelve and twenty-one were obliged to join the organization during World War II and underwent military training and service.

Lutz, Carl (1895–1975) A Swiss diplomat who rescued tens of thousands of Hungarian Jews by bringing them under Swiss protection. As vice-consul, Lutz represented the interests of countries that had closed their embassies in Hungary, including the United States and Britain. In this capacity, he issued 8,000 diplomatic letters of protection for Hungarian Jews. He then applied the number to families instead of individuals and started duplicating the numbers. It is estimated that he saved over 60,000 with these protective letters, also sharing his method with the Swedish diplomat Raoul Wallenberg. Lutz also established seventy-six safe houses in Budapest, including the Glass House, which gave thousands of Jews refuge until Budapest was liberated. In 1964, Yad Vashem recognized Carl Lutz as Righteous Among the Nations. *See also* Glass House; Wallenberg, Raoul.

Massuah Institute A museum and learning centre dedicated to research and education about the Holocaust, located in Kibbutz Tel Yitzhak in central Israel. Established in 1972 by Hanoar Hatzioni and other Zionist youth groups, the institute contains an archive, library, amphitheatre, dormitories and conference rooms, and runs events and activities for the general public, including workshops, exhibitions and meetings with Holocaust survivors. *See also* kibbutz.

National Bureau of the Jews of Hungary The umbrella organization of Hungary's Neolog congregations. *See also* Neolog Judaism.

Neolog Judaism A reform movement that emerged from the 1868 Hungarian Jewish Congress. Neolog Jews were more liberal and secular than Orthodox Jews and spoke Hungarian rather than Yiddish as their first language. In present-day Hungary, most of the small Jewish community that remains belongs to Neolog synagogues.

Országos Magyar Zsidó Segítő Akció (OMZSA; in English, National Hungarian Jewish Aid Association) An organization established by Neolog, Orthodox and Zionist leaders in 1939 to provide for the needs of Hungarian Jews in response to anti-Jewish laws and regulations.

Orthodox (Judaism) The set of beliefs and practices of Jews for whom the observance of Jewish law is closely connected to faith; it is characterized by strict religious observance of Jewish dietary laws, restrictions on work on the Sabbath and holidays, and a code of modesty in dress.

Schutzpass (German; pl. *Schutzpässe*; protective pass) A visa that identified the holder as a Swedish subject. Swedish diplomat Raoul Wallenberg issued these passes to at least 15,000 Hungarian Jews, thereby saving them from deportation. *See also* Wallenberg, Raoul.

Shabbat (Hebrew; in Yiddish, Shabbes, Shabbos) The weekly day of rest beginning Friday at sunset and ending Saturday at nightfall, ushered in by the lighting of candles on Friday evening and the recitation of blessings over wine and challah (egg bread); A day of celebration as well as prayer, it is customary to eat three festive meals, attend synagogue services and refrain from doing any work or travelling.

shamashim (plural of *shamash*; Hebrew; also *gabbaim*) Synagogue caretakers who assist with the running of synagogue services.

Siege of Budapest The battle from December 24, 1944, to February 13, 1945, between German and pro-German Hungarian troops and the Soviet Red Army and Romanian army; the latter encircled Budapest to liberate the city. Buda was liberated in mid-January; Pest, in mid-February.

SS (abbreviation of Schutzstaffel; Defence Corps) The SS was established in 1925 as Adolf Hitler's elite corps of personal bodyguards. Under the direction of Heinrich Himmler, its membership grew from 280 in 1929 to 50,000 when the Nazis came to power in 1933, and to nearly a quarter of a million on the eve of World War II. The SS was comprised of the Allgemeine-SS (General SS) and the Waffen-SS (Armed, or Combat SS). The General SS dealt with policing and the enforcement of Nazi racial policies in Germany and the Nazi-occupied countries. An important unit within the SS was the Reichssicherheitshauptamt (RSHA, the Central Office of Reich Security), whose responsibility included the Gestapo (Geheime Staatspolizei). The SS ran the concentration and death camps, with all their associated economic enterprises, and also fielded its own Waffen-SS military divisions, including some recruited from the occupied countries.

Star of David (in Hebrew, *Magen David*) The six-pointed star that is the ancient and most recognizable symbol of Judaism. During World War II, Jews in Nazi-occupied areas were frequently forced to wear a badge or armband with the Star of David on it as an identifying mark of their lesser status and to single them out as targets for persecution.

United Nations Relief and Rehabilitation Administration (UNRRA) An international relief agency created at a 44-nation conference in Washington, DC, on November 9, 1943, to provide economic assistance and basic necessities to war refugees. It was especially active in repatriating and assisting refugees in the formerly Nazi-occupied European nations immediately after World War II.

Wallenberg, Raoul (1912–1947?) The Swedish diplomat who was sent to Hungary in June 1944 by the US Refugee Board and succeeded in saving tens of thousands of Budapest Jews by issuing them Swedish certificates of protection. The Swedish government also authorized Wallenberg to set up thirty "safe houses" and organize food distribution, medical assistance and child care for Jews in Budapest. Of the slightly more than 100,000 Jews that remained alive in Budapest at the end of the war (out of a pre-war population of 247,000), the majority were saved through his efforts. Wallenberg was awarded the title of Righteous Among the Nations by Yad Vashem in 1986 and has been honoured by memorials or monuments in ten other countries.

War of Independence Also known as the 1948 Arab-Israeli War or the first Arab-Israeli War. The conflict between the state of Israel and Arab forces after Israel's independence was declared on May 14, 1948.

Yiddish A language derived from Middle High German with elements of Hebrew, Aramaic, Romance and Slavic languages, and written in Hebrew characters. Spoken by Jews in east-central Europe for roughly a thousand years from the tenth century to the mid-twentieth century, it was still the most common language among European Jews until the outbreak of World War II. There are similarities between Yiddish and contemporary German.

Zionism A movement promoted by the Viennese Jewish journalist Theodor Herzl, who argued in his 1896 book *Der Judenstaat* (The Jewish State) that the best way to resolve the problem of antisemitism and persecution of Jews in Europe was to create an independent Jewish state in the historic Jewish homeland of Biblical Israel. Zionists also promoted the revival of Hebrew as a Jewish national language.

Photographs

1 Tibor's parents, David and Helen (née Reiner) Benyovits. Budapest, circa 1920.

2 Tibor, age six, with his immediate family. Standing in back: Tibor's sister Magda (left) and his brother Jenö (right). Seated in front (left to right): Tibor's mother, Helen; Tibor; his brother Jozsef; his father, David; and his sister Edith. Budapest, circa 1938.

1   Tibor's father, David. Budapest, 1943.
2   Tibor's brother Jenö. Budapest, 1943.
3   Tibor's sister Edith, after taking on a Christian identity during the war. Budapest, 1944.
4   Tibor's brother Jozsef (Suci). Budapest, 1944.

Tibor's aunt Elza (née Reiner) and her husband, Zoltán (Zolti) Libman. Vác, Hungary, 1949.

1   Tibor (standing, far left) with friends from his Zionist youth group Hanoar
    Hatzioni before leaving for Israel. Buda Mountains, Hungary, April 1949.
2   Tibor (front, right) with members of his pilot training course. Israel, 1952.
3   Tibor's mother, Helen. Ramat HaSharon, Israel, circa 1950.
4   Yehuda Benyovits, Tibor's cousin and leader of his youth group, Hanoar Hatzioni.
    Israel, 1953.

1   Tibor on Yom Ha'atzmaut, Independence Day in Israel. 1953.

2   Tibor's fiancée, Miriam, in the Israeli army. 1953.

3   Tibor and Miriam on their wedding day. Israel, October 12, 1953.

1   The Bethlen tér synagogue in Budapest. Photo taken by Tibor in the 1970s.

2   A view of the Bethlen tér synagogue showing three memorial panels listing mem-
    bers of the shul — including Tibor's father — who died during the Holocaust.
    Photo taken by Tibor in the 1970s.

1 Edith, Tibor's sister, on the dairy farm. 1960.

2 Tibor's family visiting his sister Magda and family in Israel. Standing (in back): Magda's second husband, Heinz (left), and Magda's son, David (right). In front: Magda; Tibor's wife, Miriam; and their daughter, Ronit. Tibor's son, Amit, can be seen in the background. Ramat HaSharon, Israel, circa 1970.

1 Tibor's daughter, Ronit, and his son-in-law, Dale White. Toronto, 1992.
2 Tibor and Miriam celebrating their eightieth birthdays with their children
   and two of their grandchildren. From left to right (in back): Tibor's son, Amit;
   Miriam; Tibor; his grandson, Joshua; and his daughter, Ronit. In front, Tibor's
   granddaughter Rebecca. Toronto, 2012.
3 Tibor's granddaughter Rebecca, at age fourteen. Toronto, 2014.
4 Tibor's grandson, Joshua, upon graduation from high school. Toronto, 2014.

Tibor's granddaughter Jamie upon graduation from McMaster University. Hamilton, 2017.

Tibor on a cruise. 2010.

Tibor and Miriam. Toronto, 2018.

Index

Britain, 70

British forces, 19–20

British Mandate Palestine, 70, 75n5

Brothers for Resistance and Rescue: The Underground Zionist Youth Movement in Hungary During World War II (Gur), 1n2

Budapest. *see also* Hungary; Bethlen Synagogue, 4–6, 46–47, 49–52; bombing, 18–20, 32, 46; ghetto, 41, 42; siege of, 37–52

Budapest ghetto, xvii, 31

Budapest Jewish Youth Culture Organization, 9

Buffett, Warren, 123

Canada, 114, 115–16, 118, 119–26, 125

Catholic teachers' organization (Budapest), 67

cattle wagons, 17

Central Bureau of the Autonomous Orthodox Jewish Community, 5n3

Communist Party: growth, 68, 77–78, 84; Israel statehood reaction, 81

Cory, Sergeant Major, 104

csendőrs (gendarmes), 16–17, 24

Csepel Island, 18

Csepel Works, 18

Czechoslovakia, 84–87

Dajnus, 23, 24. *See also* Billitzer, Dr.

Daty (family friend), 7, 47–48

David (Magda's son), 99

death camps, 11, 16–17, 93

Debrecen (Hungary), 68

Deutsch, Dr., 14

DPs (displaced persons), 69–70, 72

Duna (Danube) River, 18

Dunka, László, 23. *See also* Billitzer, Dr.

Eagle's Nest (Hitler), 74

Edith (cousin), 60, 117, 119

Egypt, 87

Eichmann, Adolf, xvii

Eilat (Israel), 110

Ein Shemer kibbutz, 107

Eka (*kvutza* leader), 82–83

Ekstein, Yehuda, 104

Engel (husband of Magda Benyovits), 72, 99–100

Eretz Yisrael, 8, 68–69, 70

Eva (friend), 86

Exodus, 75n5

Extrusion Machinery Company (Toronto), 120–22

female reserves, 105

Final Solution, 16–17

forced-labour battalions, xviii–xix, 4–5, 11–12, 17n4, 27, 28, 31, 47, 59, 66

Garzo (friend), 76

General Jewish Congress, 5n3

Germany, 14–25, 73–74

Glass House, 43–44

Gordon (Zsuzsi's husband), 99, 100

Grof, Ella, 65–66

Grof, Laci, 65–66

Grof family, 28, 54–56, 64–65, 66, 77

Gur, David, 1n2

Hadassah, 96–97

Hadera (Israel), 98

Haifa, 95, 98, 117